신흥교역국의 통관환경 연구

인 도

한국조세재정연구원

2014년 11월 15일 1판 1쇄 인쇄
2014년 11월 15일 1판 1쇄 발행

지 은 이　세법연구센터 / 한국조세재정연구원
발 행 인　이헌숙
표　　지　김학용
발 행 처　생각쉼표 & 주)휴먼컬처아리랑
　　　　　서울특별시 영등포구 여의도동 45-13 코오롱포레스텔 309
전　　화　070) 8866 - 2220 FAX • 02) 784-4111
등록번호　제 2009 - 000008호
등록일자　2009년 12월 29일

www.휴먼컬처아리랑.kr
ISBN 979-11-5565-097-4

신흥교역국의 통관환경 연구

인 도

한국조세재정연구원

※ 본 보고서는 인도 관세제도의 대부분을 담기 위해서 노력하였으나 지면의 부족 및 시간상의 제약으로 인해 부족한 부분이 있다.

또한 가급적 최신의 내용을 수록하기 위하여 노력하였지만, 사회·경제 상황에 따라 세제에 변화가 빈번하여, 가장 최신의 내용을 본 보고서에 반영하는 데에는 한계가 있었다.

따라서 본 보고서는 인도의 관세에 대한 최소한의 길라잡이임을 밝히며, 보다 정확하고 구체적인 사항은 인도 관세소비세 중앙위원회 및 관세평가국의 출판물 및 홈페이지와 관련 법령을 참조할 것을 권장함. 특히 민감한 사안에 대하여는 반드시 관련 법령을 통해 확인할 필요가 있으며, 불명확한 부분에 대해서는 관련 관세전문가의 도움을 받을 것을 강조하고자 한다.

본 보고서의 내용은 저자들의 개인적인 의견이며, 한국조세연구원의 공식적인 견해와 무관함을 밝혀 둔다.

목 차

Ⅰ. 개 관··7
   1. 일반 개황··7
   2. 경제 개황··10
      가. 인도의 주요 경제 지표···10
      나. 인도의 수출입 동향···11
      다. 인도의 외국인 투자 동향···12
   3. 우리나라와 인도의 교역 관계··14
      가. 우리나라의 대(對)인도 교역현황···14
      나. 한-인도 포괄적경제제동반자협정(CEPA)···17
   4. 인도의 자유무역협정(FTA, Free Trade Agreement) 현황···············20

Ⅱ. 외국의 통상환경 보고서···22
   1. 『Doing Business 2011』상의 순위··22
   2. 미국 국별 무역장벽 보고서(National Trade Estimate Report on Foreign Trade Barriers: NTE 보고서)··23

Ⅲ. 인도의 통관 환경··27
   1. 통관 및 관세 제도··27
      가. 통관 행정 조직···27
      나. 관세의 종류 및 산정방법···28
      다. 기타 통관 관련 사항··29
   2. 수입 통관 절차···31
      가. 세관 신고 절차의 흐름··31
      나. 통관 구비서류··32

다. 수입 규제 및 비관세 장벽 ·· 32
　　3. 수출 통관 절차 ·· 34

Ⅳ. 통관 절차별 고려 사항 ·· 37
　1. 수입신고 전 서류 준비 단계 ·· 38
　　가. 통관 절차상 특이사항 ··· 38
　　나. 애로 사례 및 업무상 유의점 ·· 39
　　다. 한 – 인도 CEPA의 활용 ··· 41
　2. 수입신고 및 세관심사 단계 ·· 42
　　가. 통관 절차상 특이사항 ··· 42
　　나. 인도 세관 전자자료공유(EDI) 시스템(ICES, Indian Customs EDI System) ······ 43
　3. 특혜관세 및 면세의 적용 ·· 44
　　가. 통관 절차상 특이사항 ··· 44
　　나. 신용 공인 프로그램(ACP, Accredited Credits Programme) ··············· 45
　4. 수입신고 수리 이후 단계 ·· 47
　　가. 통관 절차상 특이사항 ··· 47
　　나. 애로 사례 및 업무상 유의점 ·· 47
　5. 수출 및 환급 단계 ·· 48
　　가. 통관 절차상 특이사항 ··· 48
　　나. 애로 사례 및 업무상 유의점 ·· 49

참고문헌 ··· 50

부 록 ·· 51
　부록 Ⅰ. Business Tip ·· 51
　부록 Ⅱ. 주요 유관 기관 정보 ··· 53
　부록 Ⅲ. 인도의 수출입 통관 절차(Procedure for Clearance of Imported and Export
　　　　　Goods) ·· 56
　부록 Ⅳ. 인도 관세법(THE CUSTOMS TARIFF ACT, 1975) ······················ 78

부록 Ⅴ. 인도 세관법(통관관련 부분) ··· 132
부록 Ⅵ. 통관 관련서류 양식 ··· 187

표 목차

〈표 Ⅰ-1〉 인도의 주요 경제 지표 ·· 10
〈표 Ⅰ-2〉 인도의 대외교역규모(2009) ·· 11
〈표 Ⅰ-3〉 인도의 주요국가별 수출입현황(2009) ······························ 12
〈표 Ⅰ-4〉 인도의 업종별 외국인직접투자 유치 현황 ························ 13
〈표 Ⅰ-5〉 인도의 국가별 외국인직접투자 유치 현황 ························ 14
〈표 Ⅰ-6〉 최근 대(對)인도 10대 수출 품목 ···································· 16
〈표 Ⅰ-7〉 최근 대(對)인도 10대 수입 품목 ···································· 17
〈표 Ⅰ-8〉 대(對)인도 주요 수출입 품목(Top 10)의 양허결과 ············ 19
〈표 Ⅰ-9〉 인도의 자유무역협정 및 경제 협력 강화 ·························· 21
〈표 Ⅱ-1〉 인도의 수출입 관련 순위 ·· 23
〈표 Ⅲ-1〉 관세 산정 방식 ·· 28
〈표 Ⅳ-1〉 통관 절차별 유의 사항 ··· 37

그림 목차

[그림 Ⅰ-1] 우리나라의 대(對)인도 수출입 물량 및 무역수지 ············ 15
[그림 Ⅲ-1] 인도 관세청 본청 조직도 ·· 27

Ⅰ. 개 관

1. 일반 개황[1]

□ 인도(The Republic of India)의 국토면적은 328만㎢로 세계에서 7번째로 넓은 면적을 가지고 있으며, 이는 남한의 약 33배에 해당함
  ○ 북서로는 파키스탄, 아프가니스탄, 북으로는 중국, 네팔, 부탄, 동으로는 미얀마, 방글라데시, 남으로는 스리랑카와 접경하고 있음
  ○ 인도는 열대 몬순 기후로 분류되며 지역에 따라 차이가 있으나, 크게 혹서기(3~6월), 우기(7~9월), 건기(10~2월)로 나누어짐

□ 국가형태는 대통령제를 가미한 의원내각제·연방제이며, 연방정부는 대통령 및 대통령에게 자문을 행하는 각료위원회(Council of Ministers)로 구성되고, 각료위원회 위원장은 총리임
  ○ 대통령은 국가원수로서 군통수권과 일체의 행정권을 보유하고 있으나 실질적인 권한은 총리가 행사함
  ○ 총리는 연방하원의 다수의석을 차지하는 정당 또는 연합세력의 지도자로 대통령이 지명함

□ 1947년 독립이후 인도의 외교정책은 비동맹주의와 균형주의로 설명할 수 있으며, 1991년 소련 붕괴 이후 비동맹운동은 정치보다는 사회·경제 및 국제관계에 초점을 두는 실용적인 노선을 취하기 시작하였음
  ○ 현재 인도는 고도 경제성장 실현, 국제원자력 협력추진을 통한 핵보유국으로서의 국제적인 위상 확보, 유엔 안보리 상임이사국 진출 추진 등 세계 강대국의 하나로

---
[1] KOTRA, 『KOTRA 新 인도 비즈니스 가이드』, 2010

급부상하고 있음

□ 중국과 더불어 세계 경제의 차세대 리더로 인정이 되고 있는 것도 사실이지만, 전체 경제를 두고 볼 때는 아직 많은 어려움이 있음
  ○ 국민의 약 19%가 절대 빈곤층에 속하고, 하루 500원 이하로 연명하는 사람이 8억명에 달하고, 연 2%가 넘는 증가율로 매년 약 1,600만명씩 인구가 증가함
  ○ 빈약한 국내 자본과 낙후된 사회 간접 시설은 경제 계획 수행에 상당한 장애 요소가 되고 있음
  ○ 그러나 정치적 안정, 외부에 크게 의존할 필요가 없는 풍부한 자원, 광범위한 산업 기반, 증가 일로에 있는 양질의 기술 인력, 경제 개방과 자유화 정책 등에 힘입어 본격적인 고도 성장 궤도에 진입하였다는 평가를 받고 있음

□ 인도의 인구는 2011년 기준 약 12억 1천만명으로 추정되고 있으며 전 세계 인구의 17.31%를 차지하는 세계 2위 인구대국이며, 이 중 도시인구 비중은 1990년대 1/4정도에서 2010년 1/3 수준으로 상승한 것으로 추정됨
  ○ 2008년 기준 연령별 인구 비율은 15~64세의 인구가 전체의 63.3%, 15세 이하의 비율은 31.5%로 저연령층이 두터운 편이기 때문에 노동집약적 제조업을 육성하는 데 장기적으로 중국보다 더 큰 잠재력이 있음

□ 인도에서는 아직도 카스트제도가 엄연히 실재하고 있음
  ○ 브라만(사제), 크샤트리아(무사), 바이샤(농민·상인 등의 서민), 수드라(노예) 등 4개의 큰 계급구조로 구분됨
  ○ 4개의 큰 계급 안에서 2,300여 개의 세부계급으로 구분되며 100여 종류의 최하급 계급이 존재하는 것으로 알려짐

□ 인도의 화폐단위는 루피(Rupee, Rs., INR)와 파이샤(Paise, P.)이며 1루피는 100파이샤이고 1루피는 약 25원임

□ 인도의 회계 연도(Fiscal Year)는 매년 4월 1일부터 익년 3월 31일까지이며 대부분의 통계 및 경제관련 자료는 09-10이나 2009-2010 혹은 FY2009와 같이 회계연도를 기준으로 표시함

□ 인도의 물가수준은 우리나라에 비해 싼 것으로 알려져 있으나 품목과 지역에 따라 큰 편차를 보이고, 경제금융의 중심지인 뭄바이 같은 대도시의 사무실 임차료, 집세 등은 세계 5위권 수준으로 서울을 상회함

□ 인도에는 수많은 휴일이 있으며 처음 투자 진출한 업체는 이러한 휴일 때문에 난처한 경우가 빈번하게 발생함
  ○ 휴일은 주에 따라 다르며, 이슬람교, 힌두교, 불교 등 다양한 종교가 반영되어 있으며 이는 이슬람력, 힌두력 등에 따라 매년 날짜가 바뀌는 휴일이 대부분임
  ○ 인도인들은 집안, 종교, 경조사 등과 관련하여 휴무를 매우 중요시하므로 유급과 무급 휴가일수, 날짜 등이 표시된 연간 '근무력'을 고용계약시 명확하게 만들어야 함

□ 인도는 영국 식민 지배시의 관습과 사회주의적 정책운영으로 전통적으로 관료의 힘이 매우 강하며 이런 유산이 아직도 사회 전반에 남아 있음
  ○ 일상생활, 인허가 취득, 사업 운영시 관료 사회와의 접촉이 필수적이며 일선 하부조직에서 고위층까지 문제해결에 많은 시간과 경제적·비경제적 비용이 소요되는 것이 일반적임
  ○ 특히 인도 투자 진출, 세관통관, 정부 공기업 입찰, 조세납부 등에 있어서는 이러한 측면에 대한 고려가 필수적임

2. 경제 개황

가. 인도의 주요 경제 지표

☐ 2000년대 들어 인도 경제는 IT부문의 급성장으로 2003~2007년 중 8~9%대의 높은 성장세를 보였으나, 국제금융위기와 세계경기 침체의 영향으로 투자 및 소비와 수출이 감소하여 성장세가 둔화되었음
  ○ 인도는 수출입 비중이 GDP의 약 40% 이하를 차지하고 있어 거대한 내수시장을 바탕으로 한 민간소비가 경제성장을 주도하고 있음
  ○ 여타 국가들에 비해 세계경기 변동의 영향을 덜 받아 경제성장률이 2008년 4.93%에서 2009년 9.10%로 빠르게 회복하고 있음

☐ 인도 주요 경제연구소인 CMIE(Center for Monitoring Economy)에 따르면, 2010-2011 회계연도의 실질경제성장률은 8.6%를 기록했으며, 2011-2012 회계연도의 경우, 9.4%의 성장세를 보일 것으로 예상함

〈표 I-1〉 인도의 주요 경제 지표

구분	2007년	2008년	2009년	2010년
경상 GDP(억달러)	12,424	12,160	13,773	17,271
1인당 GDP(달러)	1,104.59	1,066.69	1,192.08	1,474.98
경제성장률(%)	9.82	4.93	9.10	8.81
물가상승률(%)	6.37	8.35	10.88	11.99
실업률(%)	7.2	6.8	10.7	10.8
대미달러환율	41.35	43.51	48.41	45.73
수출(억달러)	2,539	2,894	2,730	3,720
수입(억달러)	3,038	3,516	3,448	4,280
FDI(순유입, 억달러)	82	241	197	110
외환보유(억달러)	2,770	2,474	2,652	2,753

자료: World Bank Database; CIA World Fact Book

□ 인도의 성장 동인으로는 고도의 경제성장을 바탕으로 한 12억 인구의 거대한 내수시장의 실질 구매력 급증과 저임의 풍부한 영어구사 노동력, 세계적인 수준의 IT산업 등을 들 수 있음

□ 반면, 다양한 종교·민족·언어 등의 복잡한 사회구조로 인한 사회 불안요인이 상존하고, 전력·교통·통신 등의 인프라가 열악하며, 심각한 관료주의와 복잡한 행정업무로 인해 행정 효율성이 낮아 인도 경제발전의 장애요소가 됨

나. 인도의 수출입 동향[2]

□ 인도의 교역규모는 2009년 3,990억달러로서 세계 16위(1.6%)이며, 수출은 1,550억달러로 세계 22위, 수입은 2,440억달러로 세계 15위를 차지하고 있음

〈표 Ⅰ-2〉 인도의 대외교역규모(2009)

(단위: 10억달러, %)

순위	국가	수출		수입		전체	
		금액	비중	금액	비중	금액	비중
1	미국	1,057	8.5	1,604	12.7	2,661	10.6
2	중국	1,202	9.6	1,106	8.0	2,208	8.8
3	독일	1,121	9.0	931	7.4	2,052	8.2
10	한국	364	2.9	323	2.6	687	2.7
16	인도	155	1.2	244	1.9	399	1.6

자료: WTO; KOTRA, 2010.

□ 인도의 주요 수출품목은 다이아몬드를 비롯한 보석류, 철광석, 농수산물, 석유 및 화학제품 등이며 주요 수입품목은 원유 및 석유제품, 기계류, 가공하지 않은 보석류 등이 차지하고 있음

---

[2] KOTRA(2010), KOTRA 국가정보 인도편 '투자환경'에서 요약, 발췌

□ 인도의 2010-11 회계연도 4월-10월 수출은 1,226억달러로 2009-10 회계연도 4월-10월 대비 28% 증가하였고, 수입은 1,919억달러로 전년 동기간 대비 24.7% 증가하였음
  ○ 교역규모는 세계경제위기를 극복하며 성장세를 유지해 2010년 4월~2011년 2월 기간 동안 1,003억달러가 증가하였음

□ 2009년도 기준 인도의 주요 수입대상국은 중국, UAE, 미국, 사우디아라비아, 호주, 이란, 독일, 스위스, 한국 순이며, 우리나라는 인도의 10위 수출대상국이며, 9위 수입대상국임

〈표 Ⅰ-3〉 인도의 주요국가별 수출입현황(2009)

(단위: 억달러, %)

순위	수 출				수 입			
	국가	금액	증가율	비중	국가	금액	증가율	비중
1	UAE	206	-15.79	12.6	중국	288	-14.34	11.44
2	미국	181	-19.23	11.06	UAE	154	-37.11	6.12
3	중국	99	-6.45	6.03	미국	146	-21.34	5.82
4	홍콩	69	-1.72	4.23	사우디아라비아	145	-37.32	5.78
5	싱가포르	65	-29.11	3.95	호주	106	-5.09	4.2
6	네덜란드	64	-1.26	3.9	이란	105	-24.66	4.19
7	미국	61	-12.12	3.76	독일	103	-13.33	4.11
8	독일	54	-14.69	3.31	스위스	102	-21.66	4.06
9	미확인국가	43	21.07	2.61	한국	77	-13.54	3.06
10	한국	37	-2.53	2.28	인도네시아	76	18.62	3.01
	전체	1,634	-16.24	100	전체	2,517	-21.7	100

자료: WTA(World Trade Association; KOTRA(2010)

다. 인도의 외국인 투자 동향[3]

□ 인도의 외국인직접투자가 크게 증가한 것은 1990년대 중반부터이며, 특히 1990년대 후반부터 인도의 IT 산업이 부각되면서 인도에 대한 선진국들의 IT투자가 증가한 것

---
3) KOTRA, 『KOTRA 국가정보 인도편』, '투자환경' 부분, 2010.

이 인도의 외국인 투자가 증가하는 계기가 됨
- ○ 인도에 대한 외국인투자는 각국의 주요기업들을 중심으로 이루어졌으며, 일반 중소기업들의 본격적인 투자는 인프라 부족 등으로 크게 증가하지 못하였음
- ○ 2009-2010 회계연도의 투자유치금액은 371억 8,200만 달러로 2008-2009 회계연도의 351억 8,000만 달러 대비 5.6% 증가하였으며, 이런 투자유입 증가추세는 세계적인 금융위기로 투자심리가 극도로 위축되는 가운데 고무적으로 평가됨

□ 여러 가지 산업 및 인프라 제약 조건과 시장특성 등으로 인해 외국인 투자는 금융업, 전자산업, 통신업 등에 집중되어 있으며, 기타 부동산 분야 및 건설업 등이 그 뒤를 따르고 있음
- ○ 금번 재집권에 성공한 UPA 연정의 최초 집권 이후, 외국인투자정책은 개방의 방향을 지속하고 있고, 이에 따라 소수 업종을 제외하고는 외국인투자가 대부분 개방, 제조업 전반은 100% 투자가 대부분 가능하도록 열려 있음

〈표 Ⅰ-4〉 인도의 업종별 외국인직접투자 유치 현황

(단위: 백만달러, %)

순위	분야	2008~2009	2009~2010	2010.4~2011.1	2000.4~2011.1	총유입액 대비 비중
1	서비스 (금융, 비금융 포괄)	6,138	4,353	2,987	26,597	21%
2	컴퓨터 SW/HW	1,677	919	708	10,644	8%
3	통신 (핸드폰, 전화서비스)	2,558	2,844	1,332	10,262	8%
4	주거 및 부동산	2,801	2,844	1,048	9,405	7%
5	건설 (도로/고속도로 포함)	2,028	2,868	1,006	9,059	7%
6	자동차	1,152	1,208	1,191	5,788	5%
7	전력	985	1,437	1,033	5,680	4%
8	야금	961	407	1,011	4,141	3%
9	석유 및 천연가스	412	272	541	3,120	2%
10	화학(비료 제외)	749	362	382	2,876	2%

자료: Ministry of Commerce & Industry; Department of Industrial Policy & Promotion

□ 대(對)인도 주요 투자국은 모리셔스, 싱가포르, 미국, 영국, 네덜란드 등이며, 인도에 대한 최대 투자국은 모리셔스로서 전체 인도 외국인투자 유치 총액의 43%를 차지하였음
  ○ 이는 모리셔스가 미국과 유럽 등 선진국의 조세회피처(Tax Haven)로 사랑받고 있기 때문으로 분석됨
  ○ 우리나라는 2000년 4월 이후 누계기준 인도의 제 15위 투자국으로 대(對)인도 외국인직접투자의 약 0.61%를 차지하고 있음

〈표 Ⅰ-5〉 인도의 국가별 외국인직접투자 유치 현황

(단위: 백만달러, %)

순위	국 가	2008년-2009년	2009년-2010년	2010.4 - 2011.1	2000.4 이후 누계액	총유입액 대비 비중
1	모리셔스	11,229	10,376	6,129	53,369	42%
2	싱가포르	3,454	2,379	1,504	11,694	9%
3	미국	1,802	1,943	1,092	9,371	7%
4	영국	864	657	503	6,387	5%
5	네덜란드	883	899	1,048	5,535	4%
6	일본	405	1,183	1,367	5,082	4%
7	키프로스	1,287	1,623	755	4,655	4%
8	독일	629	626	119	2,918	2%
9	프랑스	467	303	690	2,220	2%
10	UAE	257	629	326	1,875	1%
	총 FDI 유입액	27,331	25,834	17,080	127,369	

자료: Ministry of Commerce & Industry, Department of Industrial Policy & Promotion

3. 우리나라와 인도의 교역 관계

가. 우리나라의 대(對)인도 교역현황

□ 우리나라의 대(對)인도 교역은 2003년부터 급속히 증가하기 시작하여 2008년까지 무역수지와 교역량 모두 빠르게 증가함

○ 세계적 경기침체로 인하여 2009년 들어 수출과 수입이 각각 10.7%, 37.1% 감소하는 모습을 보였지만, 세계적 경기침체를 극복하며 2010년에는 수출과 수입이 각각 42.7%, 40.8% 증가하는 모습을 보임
○ 2010년 1월 한-인도 CEPA[4])가 공식 발효되며 인도와의 경제관계가 돈독해짐에 따라 2010년 인도와의 교역량이 급증하고 있음
  - 2010년 기준 수출은 114억달러, 수입은 57억달러를 기록하였으며, 무역수지도 지속적으로 증가하며 2010년 58억달러의 흑자를 기록하였음

[그림 Ⅰ-1] 우리나라의 대(對)인도 수출입 물량 및 무역수지

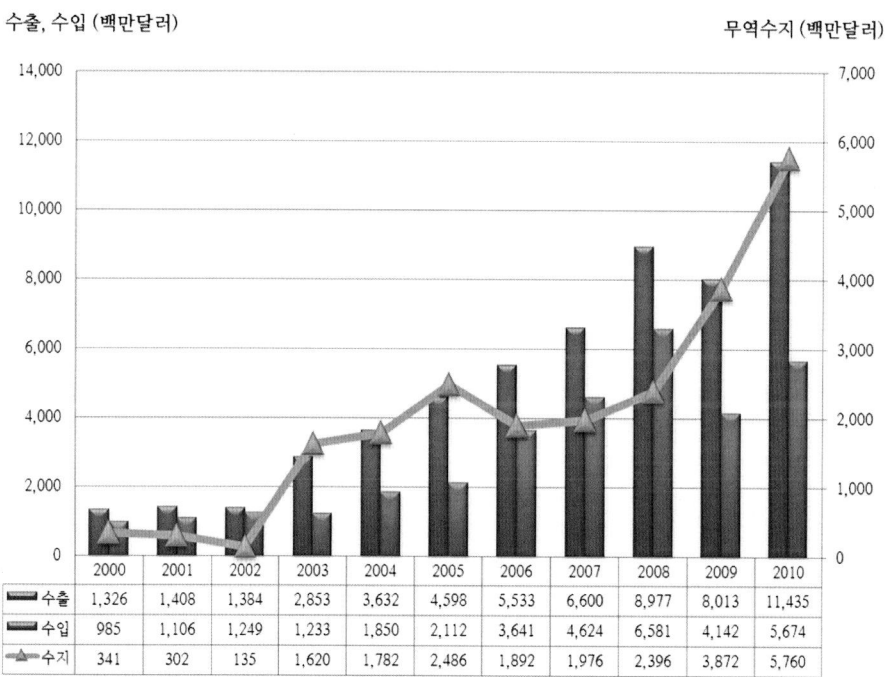

자료: 무역협회

□ 우리나라의 대(對)인도 주요 수출품목은 자동차부품, 철강판, 합성수지, 선박, 무선통

---

4) CEPA(포괄적경제동반자협정, Comprehensive Economic Partnership Agreement): 상품교역, 서비스교역, 투자, 경제협력 등 경제 관계 전반을 포괄하는 내용을 강조하기 위해 채택된 용어로써 실질적으로 자유무역협정(FTA)과 동일한 성격임

신기기 등이며, CEPA의 수혜를 받아 석유화학합성원료와 자동차부품의 수출이 큰 폭으로 증가하고 있음

□ 주요 수입 품목은 수입액 기준으로 석유제품의 수입이 전체 수입의 절반 이상으로 나타났고, 철강·면직물 순으로 나타났음
  ○ 주요 수입품목은 기초 원자재 쪽에 집중되어 있으며, 이는 자원 및 원자재 확보 차원에서 인도의 중요성이 커지고 있음을 의미함

〈표 Ⅰ-6〉 최근 대(對)인도 10대 수출 품목

(단위: 천달러, %)

순위	2010년			2011년(1월~10월)		
	품목명	금액	전년 대비 증가율(%)	품목명	금액	전년 대비 증가율(%)
	총 계	11,434,596	43	총 계	10,583,210	12
1	자동차부품	1,366,863	29	자동차부품	1,320,946	14
2	철강판	1,348,155	36	철강판	1,247,665	16
3	무선통신기기	829,660	4	무선통신기기	671,573	0
4	선박해양구조물 및 부품	739,263	143	석유제품	621,469	26
5	합성수지	737,793	37	합성수지	615,643	-2
6	석유제품	580,396	31	선박해양구조물 및 부품	480,641	-34
7	공기조절기 및 냉난방기	478,238	92	합성고무	357,432	61
8	석유화학합섬원료	309,141	192	석유화학합섬원료	333,474	34
9	합성고무	280,530	110	기타석유화학제품	249,688	10
10	기타 석유화학제품	264,568	48	건설광산기계	219,020	39

주: MTI 3단위 기준
자료: 한국무역협회, 무역통계

<표 I-7> 최근 대(對)인도 10대 수입 품목

(단위: 천달러, %)

순위	2010년			2011년(1월~10월)		
	품목명	금액	전년 대비 증가율(%)	품목명	금액	전년 대비 증가율(%)
	총 계	5,674,456	37	총 계	6,744,093	46
1	석유제품	3,065,012	34	석유제품	3,896,561	59
2	천연섬유사	335,455	67	합금철선철 및 고철	384,809	45
3	합금철선철 및 고철	310,382	232	천연섬유사	257,029	-12
4	알루미늄	197,636	431	식물성물질	225,344	77
5	식물성물질	162,334	-21	철광	191,770	139
6	정밀화학원료	120,403	18	기초유분	188,519	141
7	기초유분	103,476	147	알루미늄	185,936	22
8	아연제품	101,986	268	정밀화학원료	127,996	30
9	기타금속광물	94,517	-52	아연제품	120,769	52
10	농약 및 의약품	90,443	8	농약 및 의약품	87,742	22

주: MTI 3단위 기준
자료: 한국무역협회, 무역통계

나. 한-인도 포괄적경제동반자협정(CEPA)

□ 한-인도 포괄적경제동반자협정(CEPA, Comprehensive Economic Partnership Agreement)은 상품, 서비스 무역, 투자, 경제 협력 등 전반적인 경제관계 교류를 포괄함
  ○ 일반적 자유무역협정(FTA)에 추가하여 서비스 전문직 인력 교류, 지적 재산권 보호, 투자자 보호 등 다양한 경제활동을 포함하는 포괄적 내용의 협정임
  ○ 인도측이 자국 산업계의 우려 등 국내적 민감성을 이유로 자유무역협정(FTA)이라는 명칭 대신 CEPA라는 명칭을 선호하여 명칭이 CEPA로 확정됨
  ○ 주요내용은 ① 공산품 및 농·축산물을 포함하는 상품교역 분야, ② IT관련 서비스·금융·통신·건설·운송 등 서비스 분야, ③ 무역원활화 조치, ④ 투자분야,

⑤ 이중과세방지법 · 과학기술협력 · 관세협력 등 제도분야를 포괄함

□ 상품부문에서 한-인도 CEPA의 관세 완전철폐 비중은 수입액 기준으로 한국이 84.7%, 인도가 74.6%로 인도가 기존에 체결한 FTA 중 최대 개방수준임
   ○ 인도의 관세철폐 또는 감축 대상에는 자동차부품 · 철강 · 기계 · 화학 · 전자제품 등 우리 주력 수출품이 다수 포함되었으며, 특히 우리의 대(對)인도 10대 수출품(전체 수출액의 42.1%)은 모두 포함됨
   ○ 농산물 및 임산물에 대해서는 양국이 공히 민감성을 갖고 있음을 감안, 서로 낮은 수준에서 개방하기로 합의, 피해 발생을 방지함

□ 서비스부문에서는 양측 공히 현재 진행 중인 DDA 협상에서 제시한 수준보다 높은 수준의 자유화에 합의함
   ○ 인도의 현재 WTO 서비스 양허와 비교할 때, 통신 · 사업서비스(회계 · 건축 · 부동산 · 에너지 등) · 건설 · 유통 · 광고 · 오락문화 및 운송서비스 등 다수의 분야에서 인도 시장이 추가 개방되는 효과가 발생할 것으로 예상됨
   ○ 금융서비스 분야에서 인도는 협정 발효 후 4년간 최대 10개까지 인도에 우리나라 은행 지점 설치를 긍정적으로 고려할 것을 약속함

□ 투자의 전 단계에 걸친 내국민대우(National Treatment: NT) 보장과, 일부를 제외한 모든 부문의 투자 개방에 합의하였음
   ○ 설립과 인수 등 진입단계의 투자도 보호를 받게 되었는데, 이는 설립 후 확장 · 경영 · 영업 · 매각 등 투자를 보장하는 한-인도 투자보장협정에서 더 나아간 것으로 평가됨
   ○ 인도가 자국 FTA사상 최초로 개방을 허용하지 않은 분야만 기술하고, 그 외의 모든 분야에서 원칙적으로 외국인 투자를 허용하는 Negative방식의 자유화에 합의하여 높은 수준의 투자개방을 달성함

Ⅰ. 개관 19

〈표 Ⅰ-8〉 대(對)인도 주요 수출입 품목(Top 10)의 양허결과

순위	대(對)인도 주요 수출품					대(對)인도 주요 수입품				
	품목명 (HS 6단위)	인도 관세율	인도 양허안	'08 수출액		품목명 (HS 10단위)	우리 관세율	우리 양허안	'08 수입액	
				백만 달러	비중 (%)				백만 달러	비중 (%)
1	자동차 기타 부분품	12.5	8년내 1~5%로 감축	1,131	12.6	나프타	1	즉시철폐	3,889	59.1
2	경유(제트유)	10	10년내 50%감축	769	8.6	합금철 (페로크롬)	3	즉시철폐	201	3.1
3	무선전화기	0	0	499	5.6	대두 유박	1.8	즉시철폐	173	2.6
4	선박(탱커)	12.5	8년철폐	430	4.8	제강용의 비합금선철	2	즉시철폐	124	1.9
5	유선전화기 부분품	0	0	248	2.8	유채 유박	0	0	119	1.8
6	철및비합금강 열연강판	5	5년철폐	208	2.3	순면사	8	양허제외	98	1.5
7	신문용지	12.5	5년철폐	172	1.9	기초유분 (부타디엔)	0	0	91	1.4
8	철및비합금강 냉연강판	5	5년철폐	165	1.8	사료용 옥수수	328	8년내 50% 감축	76	1.2
9	기타가정용전자	12.5	즉시철폐	150	1.7	참깨	630	양허제외	57	0.9
10	선박(화물선)	12.5	8년철폐	133	1.5	합금철 (페로실리코 망간)	8	8년철폐	57	0.9
소계	주요 수출품			3,780	42.1	주요 수입품			4,836	73.5
합계	전체 수출			8,977	100	전체 수입			6,581	100

자료: 외교통상부

□ 한-인도 CEPA는 세계 경제의 새로운 축으로 부상하고 있는 인도와의 포괄적 FTA로서 우리나라가 일본·중국 등 다른 경쟁국보다 한 발 앞서 체결한 데 의의가 있음
  ○ 인도는 1조 2,000억달러의 GDP와 세계 2위의 인구규모를 보유하고 있는 성장 잠재력이 풍부한 국가로서 최근 지속적인 높은 성장세를 바탕으로 내수시장과 인프라 등 각종 투자수요도 함께 증가하고 있음

□ 관세청이 2001년 1월 발표한 한-인도 CEPA 발효 후 1년의 성과 보고서에 따르면, 2010년 대(對)인도 수출금액은 총 114억달러로 전년도에 비해 약 43%가 증가하였으며, 이는 전년도 우리나라 전체 수출 증가율인 28.3%를 훨씬 웃도는 수준임
　○ 수입은 CEPA 발효 전인 2009년보다 37% 증가한 57억달러였으며, 이에 무역수지는 2009년 대비 49% 증가한 58억달러의 흑자를 기록하였음

4. 인도의 자유무역협정(FTA, Free Trade Agreement) 현황

□ 인도는 세계적인 지역경제통합으로 인해 블록화 현상이 심화됨에 따라 여기서 소외됨으로써 발생할 수 있는 불이익을 최소화하고, 오히려 적극적인 통합의 주체가 되는 것을 고려하고 있음
　○ 2000년 이전 인도의 자유무역협정은 스리랑카와의 FTA가 유일하며 방글라데시·네팔·부탄 등 주변 최빈국에 대한 특혜무역협정이 경제협력의 중요한 부분이었으나, 2000년 이후 FTA에 대한 입장을 수정함
　○ 중국이 ASEAN과의 FTA체결을 통해 이 지역에 영향력을 키우고 있는데 중국의 동남아시아에 대한 경제적 영향력이 급속하게 확장됨으로써 이를 견제할 수단이 필요하게 됨

□ 관세 인하 등을 통한 무역 자유화 이외에 자유무역협정 체결에도 적극적이어서, 동시다발적 FTA 체결을 추진 중임
　○ ASEAN과 한·중·일·호주·뉴질랜드를 포함하는 FTA가 논의되면서 인도가 소외당할 위험이 커짐에 따라 인도는 2004년 태국과 FTA를, 2005년 싱가포르와 CECA(포괄적 경제협력 협정, Comprehensive Economic Cooperation Agreement)를 개별적으로 체결함
　○ 2009년 UPA 정부 2기가 들어서면서 2009년 8월에 한국과의 CEPA를, ASEAN과의 상품분야 FTA를 각각 체결함
　○ 2011년 2월, 일본과 상품 및 서비스 교역·투자·경제협력 등 전반에 걸친 경제적

교류를 위해 CEPA를, 말레이시아와 경제적 협력을 포함해 서비스와 투자 등의 영역까지 포괄하는 CECA를 체결함

<표 Ⅰ-9> 인도의 자유무역협정 및 경제 협력 강화

기 체결된 FTA	협상 중인 FTA	검토 중인 FTA
SAFTA(South Asian Free Trade Agreement) 인도-ASEAN FTA 인도-MERCOSUR PTA 인도-네팔 Treaty of Trade 인도-부탄 TA 인도-스리랑카 FTA 인도-싱가포르 CECA 인도-아프가니스탄 PTA 인도-칠레 PTA 인도-한국 CEPA 인도-일본 CEPA 인도-말레이시아 CECA	BIMST[1]-EC 인도-EFTA TIA 인도-EU FTA 인도-GCC[2] FTA 인도-SACU[3] PTA 인도-모리셔스 CECPA 인도-태국 CECA	IBSA[4] 남아프리카공화국(FTA) 뉴질랜드(FTA) 대만(FTA) 러시아(CECA) 스위스 우루과이(FTA) 이란(FTA) 이스라엘(PTA) 이집트(FTA) 인도네시아(FTA) 중국(FTA) 캐나다(CEPA) 터키(FTA) 파키스탄(FTA) 호주(FTA)

주: 1) 벵골만 포괄적경제협력체(BIMST, Bangladesh India Myanmar Sri Lanka Thailand Economic Cooperation): 방글라데시·미얀마·스리랑카·태국·부탄 등
2) 걸프 협력회의(GCC, Gulf Cooperation Council): 사우디아라비아·쿠웨이트·아랍에미리트·카타르·오만·바레인 등 6개국
3) 남아프리카 관세동맹(SACU, Southern African Customs Union): 남아프리카공화국·보츠와나·레소토·스와질랜드 등
4) 입사(IBSA, India - Brazil - South Africa)
자료: 한국무역협회, 2011.

□ 현재 인도는 대(對)인도 1위 투자국인 모리셔스와 CECA를 추진하고 있고, 방글라데시와는 2003년 협상을 개시하였으나 아직 합의에 이르지 못하고 있으며, 중국·EU와 협상을 진행하고 있음

Ⅱ. 외국의 통상환경 보고서

1. 『Doing Business 2011』상의 순위

□ 세계은행(The World Bank)은 2004년부터 매년 '사업하기 좋은 나라(Ease of doing business)' 순위를 다양한 부문에 걸쳐 조사하여 『Doing Business』라는 보고서명으로 발표하고 있음
  - ○ 2011년에 발간된 당해 보고서는 2010년 한 해 동안 183개국에 대하여 부문별로 조사·평가한 내용을 수록함
  - ○ 『Doing Business 2011』 보고서상 순위를 결정짓기 위하여 조사된 분야는 사업 개시(Starting a business), 건설 허가(Dealing with construction permit), 재산권 등록(Registering property), 신용 취득(Getting credit), 투자자 보호(Protecting investors), 세금 납부(Paying taxes), 무역(Trading across borders), 계약 이행(Enforcing contract) 및 폐업(Closing a business) 등 9개의 지표임
  - ○ 2011년 보고서에 따르면, 종합적인 '사업의 용이성(Ease of Doing Business)' 순위에 있어 싱가포르가 1위를 차지하였으며, 우리나라는 16위에 랭크되었음

□ 당해 보고서의 무역 분야 순위는 수출입에 필요한 서류의 개수와 수출입 소요 일수 및 소요 비용 등을 산출하여 순위를 정하고 있으며, 필요서류가 적고 수출입 소요 기일이 짧을수록 더욱 높은 순위에 오르는 형식임
  - ○ 무역 분야에서 우리나라는 2010년 보고서에 이어 2011년 보고서에서도 8위를 기록하며 상위권을 유지하였음

□ 세계은행(The World Bank)의 연간 보고서인 『Doing Business 2011』에 따르면 인도는 전반적인 사업의 용이성에 있어 전체 조사국인 183국 중 134위에 랭크되어 비교

적 사업을 하기에 어려운 것으로 조사되었음
- ○ 부문별 주요 지표 중 무역 분야(Trading Across Borders)에서는 이전년도인 2010년 93위에서 하락한 100위를 기록함

〈표 Ⅱ-1〉 인도의 수출입 관련 순위

구분	인도	East Asia & Pacific	OECD	브라질	중국	한국
수출필요서류(개수)	8	6.4	4.4	8	7	3
수출소요시간(일)	17	22.7	10.9	13	21	8
수출소요비용(달러/컨테이너)	1,055	889.8	1,058.7	1,790	500	790
수입필요서류(개수)	9	6.9	4.9	7	5	3
수입소요시간(일)	20	24.1	11.4	17	24	7
수입소요비용(달러/컨테이너)	1,025	934.7	1,106.3	1,730	545	790
무역분야 순위	100	-	-	114	50	8

자료: The World Bank, 『Doing Business 2011』

- ○ 인도에서 해상 수출 비용은 컨테이너당 약 1,055달러의 금액이 소요되는 것으로 조사되었으며, 수출에 필요한 서류는 8가지이고, 서류 준비를 비롯하여 수출 통관 및 국내 운송, 항만업무 등, 수출에 총 17일이 소요되는 것으로 조사되었음
- ○ 해상 수입에 있어서 컨테이너당 약 1,025달러의 금액이 소요되며, 수입에 필요한 서류는 9가지이고, 서류 준비를 포함한 수입통관 및 국내 운송, 항만 업무를 포함하여 총 20일이 소요됨

2. 미국 국별 무역장벽 보고서(National Trade Estimate Report on Foreign Trade Barriers: NTE 보고서)

□ 국별 무역장벽보고서는 1974년 통상법(Trade Act of 1974) 제181조에 근거하여 미국 무역 대표부(USTR)가 작성, 매년 3월 말 의회에 제출하는 연례 보고서임

- ○ 이 보고서는 미국 업계의 의견과 해외 주재 미국 대사관의 보고서와 관련 정부 부처의 의견 등을 기초로 작성됨
- ○ 2011년 보고서는 미국의 62개 주요 교역국 및 경제권의 무역과 투자 장벽에 대해 포괄적으로 기술하고 있음[5]

□ 미국 무역 대표부(USTR)는 인도 정부의 지속적인 경제 개혁에도 불구하고 아직도 자유로운 수입을 방해하는 수많은 관세와 비관세 장벽이 존재함을 지적함
- ○ 양국간 정책 포럼을 통해 5개의 포커스 그룹(농업·지적재산권과 같은 혁신과 창의성 부문·투자·서비스·관세)이 정기적으로 활동을 지속하고 있음
- ○ 정보통신기술 워킹그룹(the Information Communication Technology Working Group)과 같은 다른 양자 협의도 지속되어 실질적인 무역을 증대시키는 효과를 나타내고 있음

□ 인도는 복잡한 관세구조를 가지고 있으며, 기본관세·부가관세(상계관세)·특별부가관세(특별상계관세)·교육세로 구성됨
- ○ 부가관세는 와인 등과 같은 알코올 음료를 제외한 다른 모든 수입품에 적용되는 관세로서 기본관세에 더해지며, 국내 제품의 소비세(CENVAT, Central Value Added Tax)에 대응하기 위한 것임
- ○ 특별부가관세는 면세 품목을 제외한 모든 수입품에 적용되는 4%의 종가세(ad valorem)임

□ 세관이 관세 정보를 공개함에도 불구하고 수입업자들은 수입물품에 적용되는 정확한 관세를 산출하기 위해 다른 세관에 교차 확인(cross-reference)을 해야 함
- ○ 이러한 인도의 복잡한 관세구조 및 산정방식은 비관세 장벽의 하나로 작용하며, 이런 과정에서 투명성의 결여와 수입업자의 부담이 문제점으로 지적됨

---

[5] 2010년부터 SPS(동식물 위생 및 검역) 및 TBT(무역에 대한 기술 장벽) 관련 사안은 NTE 보고서와 별도로 발표하고 있음

□ 인도의 관세 당국은 또한 WTO규정에 따라 일반적으로 초과할 수 없는 양허관세율(Bound Tariff Rates)과 실제로 부과되는 실행관세율(Applied Tariff Rates)이 일치하지 않는 것으로 알려짐
- ○ WTO에 따르면, 인도의 평균 양허관세율은 2009년도 기준 48.6%였으나, 최혜국대우(MFN) 관세율은 모든 물품을 대상으로 12.9%였음
- ○ 이러한 양허관세율과 실제관세율의 차이로 인해 인도로 수출하는 기업들은 상당한 불확실성에 직면하고 있음
- ○ 인도는 모든 농산물에 대해 WTO 내의 양허관세기준을 갖고 있으나, 30%이상의 비농산물은 아직 양허관세기준을 갖고 있지 않음

□ 인도의 농산물에 대한 양허관세율은 100%에서 300%로 세계에서 가장 높은 수준이며, 평균 114.2%임
- ○ 인도의 농산물에 대한 실행관세율은 2009년 기준 32%로 낮았지만, 아직도 농산물과 가공식품 무역의 큰 장벽으로 존재함

□ 인도는 비관세 장벽의 하나로 수입규제목록(negative list)을 유지하고 있으며 크게 금지품목, 제한품목, 관심품목 등 세 가지로 분류됨
- ○ 금지품목: 수지, 지방, 동물성 기름
- ○ 제한품목: 축산물, 특성화학물
- ○ 관심품목: 석유제품, 특정 의약품

□ 통관 환경과 관련하여 세관이 수입거래에 대해 부과하는 관세 평가기준에 대해 꾸준히 의문을 제기함
- ○ 수입물품이 인도 내에서 통상 거래되는 제품의 가격보다 낮을 경우 수입물품의 통관 자체를 거부하는 경우가 있음
- ○ 미국의 수출업자들이 인도 세관의 관세평가 방법이 실제거래가치를 반영하지 못하고, 실행관세율 이상의 수출비용을 야기한다고 보고함
- ○ 컴퓨터 제품 및 부품을 수입할 때, 광범위한 관세 평가로 인하여 과도하게 검색 또

는 압류되는 경우가 발생함

□ 인도 세관 직원들은 일반적으로 과도한 서류를 요구하여 수입의 자유로운 흐름을 방해하고, 통관 처리 지연으로 이어진다고 지적함
  ㅇ 이러한 과도한 서류는 물품, 사용자, 사용목적에 따른 복잡한 관세구조와 산정방식, 다양한 면세 기준 때문인 것으로 분석됨
  ㅇ 이러한 불편이 계속되는 가운데, 인도 세관은 무역 절차의 자동화를 통하여 지속적으로 문제점을 개선하고 있음

Ⅲ. 인도의 통관 환경

1. 통관 및 관세 제도

가. 통관 행정 조직

□ 인도 관세청 조직의 공식명칭은 관세소비세 중앙위원회(CBEC: Central Board of Excise and Customs)이며, 재무부(Ministry of Finance) 산하 조세청(Department of Revenue)의 구성 조직임

□ 관세소비세 중앙위원회의 주요 업무는 관세 및 중앙소비세 부과 징수에 관한 정책 입안 밀수단속, 관세·소비세 및 마약과 관련한 행정업무 처리이며, 세관·중앙소비세 부서·중앙재정 통제분석소를 포함한 산하기관을 관리감독함

[그림 Ⅲ-1] 인도 관세청 본청 조직도

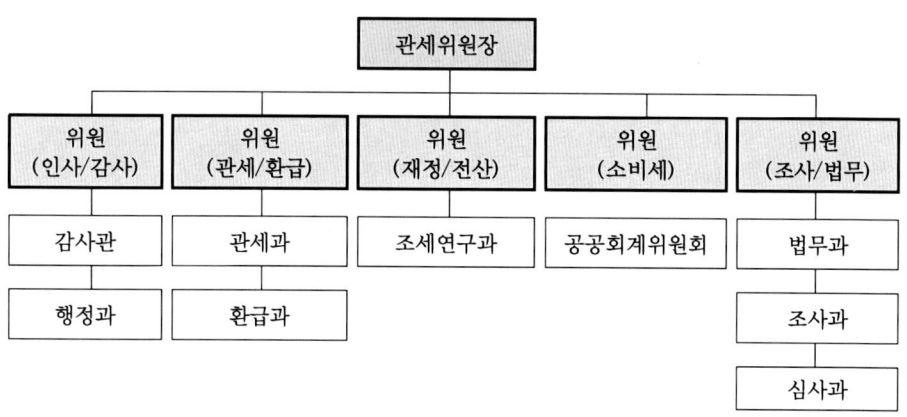

자료: 관세청(2011)

나. 관세의 종류 및 산정방법[6]

□ 관세정책은 재무부 관세소비세 중앙위원회(Central Board of Excise and Customs)가 결정하며 관세율은 관세율법(Customs Tariff Act, 1975)을 기초로 하여 매년 예산안 국회 제출시 결정됨

□ 인도의 수입 관세는 기본관세(Basic Duty)와 부가관세(Additional Duty, 상계관세라고도 함), 특별부가관세(Special Countervailing Duty, 특별상계관세라고도 함) 그리고 교육세(Educational Cess)로 구성됨

□ 2010년의 경우, 일반 품목의 기본관세율은 7.5~10%이며, 부가관세는 일반적으로 10%, 특별부가관세는 4%, 교육세는 3%임
  ○ 기본 관세율과 상계 관세율은 관세소비세 중앙위원회(Central Board of Excise and Customs) 홈페이지에서 확인할 수 있음(http://www.cbec.gov.in)
  ○ 어떤 품목의 기본관세가 10%, 부가관세가 8%, 교육세는 3%, 특별상계관세가 4%라면 산출방식은 아래와 같고, 총관세는 24.21%임

〈표 Ⅲ-1〉 관세 산정 방식

구분	세율	산식	세율
A(기본관세)	10	100	10.000
B(부가관세)	8	(100+A) × 8%	8.800
C(교육세 적용-1)	3	B × 3%	0.264
D(교육세 적용-2)	3	(A+B+C) × 3%	0.572
E(특별상계관세)	4	(100+A+B+C+D) × 4%	4.785
총관세		A+B+C+D+E	24.421

자료: KOTRA, 2010

---

[6] 무역협회(2011), 국가별 지식 '수출입 제도'에서 요약, 발췌

□ 인도는 주변국인 파키스탄·스리랑카·네팔·방글라데시 등 서남아 국가 연합 (SAARC) 국가들과 특혜관세 협정을 맺고 이들 국가에 대해서는 품목에 따라 관세 면제 또는 감면 혜택을 주고 있음

□ 태국과 FTA협상을 타결하고 2004년 11월부터 82개 품목에 대해 조기 인하 조치(Early Harvest)하였으며, 2005년 8월부터 싱가포르와 자유무역협정(CECA)을 전면적으로 발효하여 실시하고 있음

□ 중국과는 자유무역(FTA)을 추진한다는 기본원칙에 합의하고, 이를 구체화하기 위해 양국의 공동 연구 그룹이 현재 구체적인 일정을 포함한 실천 계획을 수립하고 있는 상황이며, 아세안 및 한국과는 CEPA(포괄적 경제협력 협정)를 체결하고 2010년 1월 1일부터 발효하였음

다. 기타 통관 관련 사항

□ 인도에서 일반적인 경우 통관에 소요되는 시간은 해상 운송 수입은 약 5 근무일, 항공 운송은 약 2~3근무일이 소요됨
  ○ 일반 품목이 아닌 경우(SEZ[7], EPC[8] 물품 등)는 1~2일이 추가 소요되며, 중고 기계류인 경우는 10일 이상 소요됨
  ○ 세관은 일반적으로 화물 도착 후 7일 이후부터는 체화료(demmurage charge)를 부과하는데 컨테이너 운송인 경우 5일 이후부터, 항공운송인 경우 3일 이후부터 체화료를 부과함

□ 통관시스템을 현대화하여 과거에 비해 많이 개선되었다고는 하나, 아직도 인도는 통관 절차가 복잡하고, 통관 에이전트와 세관 공무원 간의 관계가 관세액 및 통관에 영향을 미침

---

7) SEZ: Special Economic Zone, 특별경제구역
8) EPC: Export Promotion Capital, 수출촉진용 자본재

○ 통관 업무는 현지 통관사(Customs Clearing Agent)를 통해서 이루어지는데 원활한 통관을 위해 추가비용을 지불하는 경우가 있음
○ 사소한 서류 기재 오류 등을 이유로 통관이 장기간 지연되는 경우가 있음

☐ 인도 행정은 전반적으로 불투명하고 실무선의 재량권이 큰 편이며, 통관 역시 융통성 없는 처리 관행으로 인해 기업들의 주요 애로사항 중 하나로 꼽히고 있음
○ 송장(Invoice)상의 가격과소평가(Under Value)를 문제삼아 직권으로 상품 가치를 정하고 높은 관세를 매긴다거나, 관세 혜택이 주어지는 상품의 경우 증빙이 충분치 않다는 이유로 통관을 거부하는 사례 등이 발생하고 있음
○ 투자기업의 국내 모기업 제품 조달과 관련해서 이전가격의 조정을 이용한 법인세 과소 납부를 방지하기 위해 이전 가격과 관련된 각종 증빙을 수시 및 임의적으로 세관에서 요구하기도 함

☐ 인도는 통관 인프라의 부족, 관료주의 등으로 통관 절차가 필요 이상 복잡하다는 지적을 받아 왔으나, 최근 정부가 통관 제도 개선을 위해 필요한 서류 및 절차를 간소화해 가는 추세임

2. 수입 통관 절차

가. 세관 신고 절차의 흐름

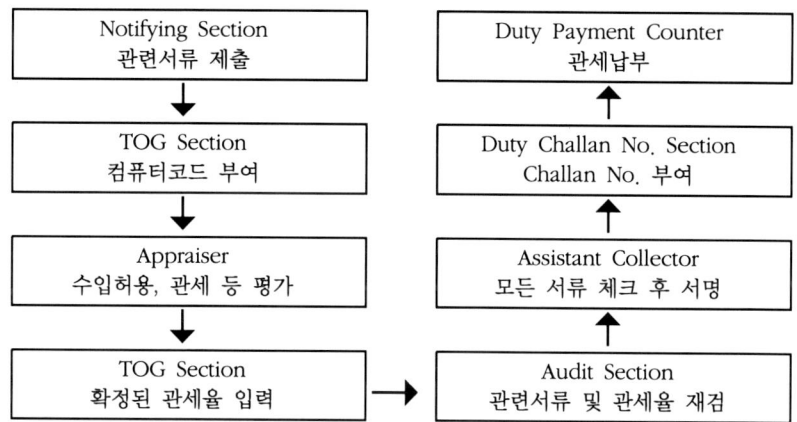

- Notifying Section : 모든 관련서류를 Notifying Officer에 제출. Officer는 Bill of Entry, Custom warehouse 측의 Manifest copy와 비교 확인
- TOG Section : 컴퓨터에 입력하고 computer code no. 부여, 관세율 등이 확정된 후 컴퓨터에 입력
- Appraiser(세관감정관) : 관련서류는 Appraiser에게 넘겨진 후 적정관세 부과 여부 등 평가
- Audit Section(검사): 관련 서류 및 관세 등을 재검
- Assistant Collector of Customs : 모든 서류를 세관의 Assistant Collector가 체크한 후 확인 서명
- 관세 Challan No. 부여
- Duty Payment Counter(관세 납부 카운터) : 관세를 납부하면 세관은 통관신고서(Bill of Entry) 사본을 1장 떼어내고 물품 수령증을 발급

나. 통관 구비서류

☐ 인도 세관을 통해 통관하기 위해서는 신용장 개설시, 수입화물의 통관시, 바이어가 통관시에 따라 각각 다른 서류들이 필요함

- ○ 신용장 개설시 은행 제출 서류
  - 수출입 허가번호[IEC(Importer-Exporter Code) No.]
  - 구매 오더(Purchase Order)
  - 송장(Invoice)
  - 공급업체 이름(Supplier's Name)
  - 공급자 거래은행명(Name of Supplier's Banker)
  - 인증서가 필요한 경우, 해당 인증서
- ○ 수입 화물의 통관시 필요 서류
  - 공급업자가 바이어에게 보낼 서류
  - 선하 증권(B/L 또는 Air-way Bill No.)
  - 송장 사본(Invoice Copy)
  - 보험 증권(Insurance Policy)
- ○ 바이어가 통관 시 준비 서류
  - 수입코드 번호(Importer's Code No.)
  - 수입신고(Import Declaration along with Bill of Entry)
  - GATT Declaration
  - 인증서가 필요한 경우, 인증서

다. 수입 규제 및 비관세 장벽[9]

☐ 인도는 2001년 기존의 수입 수량규제를 전면 철폐한 이후 수입에 있어 별다른 제한을 가하지 않고 있으며, 대부분의 품목이 OGL(Open General License) 대상으로 소정의 절차를 마치면 누구나 쉽게 수입할 수 있음

---

[9] KOTRA(2010), KOTRA 국가정보 인도편 '수입규제제도'에서 요약, 발췌

□ 인도의 품질인증 및 공업 표준규격을 부여하는 제도로는 BIS(Bureau of Indian Standard)제도가 있으며, 현재까지 표준이 의무화되어 있는 품목은 81개 품목에 불과하고 나머지는 임의 규격임
   ○ BIS 인가 신청자들은 신청 수수료·수속료·현장 방문 관련 경비·테스트 비용·인가서 관련 비용을 모두 부담해야 하기 때문에 수출을 저해하는 무역장벽으로 작용함

□ 식품에 대한 까다로운 유효기간 기준도 비관세 장벽의 하나로 작용함
   ○ 수입 당시 식품의 유효 기간은 본래 제품 수명의 60% 이상이 남아 있어야 하며, 제품수명은 제조일과 유효기간 만료일을 토대로 산출하는데 이러한 규정은 인도 국내산 제품과 비교하여 수입산 제품에 대한 차별적인 장애요소임

□ 라벨링 규정도 비관세 장벽 중의 하나이며, 소매를 목적으로 인도에 수입되는 모든 제품들은 중량 및 측정 기준규정(Standard of Weights and Measures Rules)의 조항들을 준수해야 함
   ○ 통관 전 루피화로 표시된 최고 소매가(Maximum Retail Price, MRP)를 라벨에 명시하는 것은 대(對)인도 수출업자들에게 부담으로 작용하며 라벨에 명시된 제품 가격은 세금 산출 근거로 활용됨
   ○ 대부분의 경우 판매업자들은 최고가를 실판매가로 간주하기 때문에 정확한 최고가 예측이 중요함
      − 한번 정해진 MRP는 수정할 수 없으며, 가격을 인상하기 위해서는 새로운 통관 물량부터 인상이 가능함

□ 바이어의 구매 거부로 인하여 세관에서 수출품 재반출을 거부하는 사례가 발생하기도 함
   ○ 운송된 제품에 대해 바이어가 구매를 거부할 경우, 수출자는 제3의 바이어에게 판매하거나 아니면 수출지로 재반출해야 하나, 이 경우 인도 세관에서는 원래 계약자(바이어)의 NOC(Non Objection Certification)을 요구함

- 바이어가 이러한 점을 악용해 NOC를 써 주지 않을 경우 재반출이 불가함
  ○ 바이어가 이런 현실을 악용해 시황이 안좋거나 자신에게 불리할 경우 구매를 거부한 후, 수출자의 재반출이 곤란해진 틈을 이용해 재협상을 시도하여 매우 유리한 조건으로 물품을 인도받는 경우가 종종 있음

□ 수입 식품들에 대하여 인도 관세청은 샘플 테스트를 실시하고 있지만 인증받는 시간이 오래 걸리며, 샘플링 테스트를 실시할 만한 실험실도 부족하고 추가적인 비용도 발생함
  ○ 인증을 받는 시간이 오래 걸리며, 샘플링 테스트를 실시할 만한 실험실도 부족하기 때문에 제품들은 검사를 받기 위해 유료 보관 창고에 장시간 방치되어 있으며, 일부 창고는 식품 보관에 적합하지 않은 상태임
  ○ 실험실의 검사 결과에는 이견을 제시할 수 없으며, 검사 기간에 대한 규정도 없으며, 제품 구분을 정확히 하지 못해 잘못된 기준으로 검사를 실시하는 경우도 있음

3. 수출 통관 절차

□ 수출업자는 수출상품의 통관을 위해서 선적서류를 작성하기 전에 반드시 사업인증번호(PAN[10] based BIN[11]), 수출입자코드(IEC[12])를 인도 상공부 무역국(Directorate General of Foreign Trade)으로부터 발급받아야 함
  ○ EDI 시스템상에서는 사업인증번호가 무역국 온라인 시스템으로부터 세관의 시스템으로 전송됨
  ○ 수출업자는 또한 인증된 외환 딜러 코드를 등록해야 하고, 환급 보증을 위해 지정된 은행의 계좌를 열어야 함

---

10) PAN: Permanent Account Number
11) BIN: Business Identification Number
12) IEC: Importer Exporter Code

□ 수출촉진계획 하에 수출하려고 하는 모든 수출업자는 세관에 등록된 관세 면제 자격 증명서(DEEC, Duty Exemption Entitlement Certificate Book)를 발급받아야 하고, 등록하기 위해서는 원본 서류가 필요함

□ 선적 전 필요서류는 수출업자가 관계 기관이나 부서에 발급을 신청하고, 인증받은 후 제출해야 하는 서류로서 일반적으로 상품이 수출을 위해 준비되고 실제로 선적하기 전에 구비되어야 하는 서류를 말함
  ○ 선적 전 필요서류는 송장, 포장내역서, GR form[13](원본과 사본), AR-1 form[14](원본과 사본), 수출명령서 사본, 신용장, 선하증권, 수출면허, 원산지 증명서, 검사증명서 및 기타서류임

□ 선적 후 필요서류는 주요 선적 전 서류의 인증본과 신용장을 통한 대금 지불 또는 지정은행을 통한 대금지불내용을 외국 구매자에게 보여주기 위해 선적의 증거가 은행에 제공될 수 있도록 하는 기타추가서류로 구성됨
  ○ 선적 후 필요서류는 세관증명 송장, 세관증명 포장내역서, 수출명령서 사본, 신용장 사본, 상업송장, 선하증권, 원산지 증명서, 검사 증명서, 환어음 수표 및 GR form으로 구성됨

□ EDI 시스템을 사용하지 않는 경우, 선하증권을 송장·AR-4 form[15]·포장내역서와 함께 제출하면 수출부서 평가직원에 의해 상품의 가격·분류·환급규정·적용관세·물품의 수출가능여부 등이 확인된 다음 감정사에 의해 서류와 물품이 검사된 후에 수출이 승인됨

□ EDI 시스템을 사용하는 경우, '시스템에 등록된 자료의 인증을 위한 체크리스트가 생성 → 인증 후 자료가 세관 서비스센터에 제출되고, 선하증권 번호를 수령 → 수출품

---

13) GR form: Exchange Control Declaration form(부록 IV-1 참고)
14) AR-1 form: Application for Removal of Excisable goods on payment of duty(부록 IV-2 참고)
15) AR-4: Application for removal of excisable goods for export by(Air/Sea/Port/Land) (부록 IV-3 참고)

목에 대하여 과세, 납부 → 세관 직원이 감정사와 함께 EDI상의 내용과 실제 선적물품을 비교, 확인 및 검사 → 수출 승인'의 순서로 진행됨

☐ 수출 승인 후에 선하증권이 세관용과 수출업자용으로 2부가 발급되고, 선하증권과 검사보고서에 세관의 확인 서명이 완료된 후, 감정사가 선하증권 2부에 각각 서명을 하고 도장을 찍음으로 절차가 완료됨

Ⅳ. 통관 절차별 고려 사항[16]

〈표 Ⅳ-1〉 통관 절차별 유의 사항

단계	유의 사항
1. 수입신고 전 서류 준비	○ 서류의 기재오류나 서류 상호간 불일치를 수정하기가 매우 어렵기 때문에 서류작성을 철저히 해야 함 ○ 컨테이너 별로 포장명세서와 인보이스를 작성해야 함 ○ 수입업자와 협의하여 통관업체를 지정하는 것이 효율적임 ○ 인도 정부는 신용장 방식으로 수입할 경우 보험가입 여부를 철저히 점검하기 때문에 보험가입을 반드시 점검해야 함 - 인도에서는 CIF조건 수입은 허용되지만, C&F조건 수입시에는 문제가 발생할 소지가 많음 ○ 인도는 항만, 도로 등의 인프라가 낙후돼 있고 운송수단도 노후하기 때문에 내륙운송과정에서 사고가 자주 발생하기 때문에 내륙운송보험에 가입해야 함 ○ EDI 시스템 상에서 통관이 된 경우, 공식적인 통관신고서는 전산 상에 생성되기 때문에 필요치 않지만 소정의 세부사항을 가진 화물의 통관을 위해서는 통관신고서가 필요함

2. 수입신고	○ HS 코드 분류는 인도내 수입업자와 협의하여 면밀히 검토해야 함
	○ 세관 전자자료공유(EDI)시스템의 활용
	  - 수출입업자, 통관대리인 등은 관련 서류를 전산으로 제출하며, 최종 단계의 물품의 검사와 물품의 인도 시기 외에 세관에 나올 필요가 없음
	○ 자회사-모회사와 같이 수입자와 수출자가 특수관계일 때, SVB Questionnaire를 작성하여 제출해야 함
	  - 해당 서류를 작성하여 제출할 경우 1%의 Extra Duty Deposit(보증금)을 지불하게 되며, 30일 내에 해당 서류를 작성하여 제출하지 않을 경우 5%까지 Extra Duty Deposit이 상향조정됨

3. 심사 및 분류 (특혜관세, 면세 포함)	○ 신용공인 프로그램(ACP)제도의 활용 - 신용이 공인된 수입업자에 의해 수입되는 예상 수입화물의 규모에 맞추어 세관은 별도의 시설을 만들 수 있으며, 세관의 국장은 급속한 통관을 위해 별도의 저장 공간, 처리시설 등을 제공함
4. 관세 확정 및 납부	○ 관세 확정 이후 8일을 초과하면 관세 납부 연체료를 연간 20% 복리로 부과함 - 관세를 즉시 납부하기 어려운 경우, 관세사를 통해 관세확정을 지연시키면 연체료를 절감할 수 있음
5. 물품 반출 및 환급	○ 초과 정박시 국제 관례와 다르게 내용물도 반환하지 않고, 오히려 초과정박비용을 컨테이너 소유주에게 부과함 - 수입한 화주가 나타나지 않아 항만 당국이 컨테이너를 1년 이상 묶어둔 사례도 있음

---

16) Central Board of Excise and Customs - Government of India, 『Customs Manual 2011』

1. 수입신고 전 서류 준비 단계

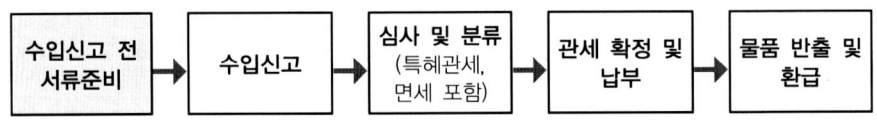

가. 통관 절차상 특이사항

□ 수입보고서 또는 수입품 목록에 인도 밖의 다른 곳이나 인도 내의 다른 세관으로 단순히 환적하는 물품의 경우에는 관세를 부과하지 아니하고, 최종 도착하는 세관에서 통관 절차를 시행함(Section 52 to 56 of the Customs Act, 1962)

□ 수입자는 관세 지불 후 인도 국내에서 물품을 소비할 것인지 즉각적인 관세 지불 없이 창고에 보관할 것인지 선택할 수 있으며, 선택한 목적에 따라 다른 색의 별도의 통관보고서를 작성해 제출해야 함(Section 46 of the Customs Act, 1962)

□ 수입자는 수입 물품에 대한 통관신고서를 작성하기 전에 무역 담당관(Directorate General of Foreign Trade)로부터 수입자 코드(IEC, Importer-Export Code)를 발급받아야 하며, 세관 전자자료공유(EDI, Electronic Data Interchange) 시스템에서 무역담당관으로부터 받은 수입자 코드가 온라인으로 등록됨

□ EDI 시스템 상에서 통관이 된 경우, 공식적인 통관신고서는 전산상에 생성되기 때문에 필요치 않지만 소정의 세부사항을 가진 화물의 통관을 위해서는 통관신고서가 필요함

□ EDI 시스템을 통하지 않는 경우에는 4부의 통관신고서를 준비하여 2부는 세관에, 1부는 송금 은행에 제출하고, 1부는 수입업자가 보관함
  ○ 통관신고서와 함께 제출하는 서류는 일반적으로 아래와 같음

- 송장(Signed invoice)
- 물품 리스트(Packing list)
- 선하증권 또는 화물인도지시서(Bill of Lading or Delivery Order/Airway Bill)
- GATT 관세평가 신고서(GATT valuation declaration)
- 수입자 신고서[Importers/CHA(Customs House Agents)'s declaration]
- 수입면허(Import license), 필요한 경우
- 신용장(Letter of Credit), 필요한 경우
- 보험서류(Insurance document)
- 산업면허(Industrial License), 필요한 경우
- 시험 결과(Test report), 화학제품과 같은 경우
- 관세 면제 자격 증명서 원본(DEEC, Duty Exemption Entitlement Certificate Book/DEPB, Duty Entitlement Passbook Scheme), 적용 가능한 경우
- 카탈로그(Catalogue), 화학물품이나 기계와 같은 경우 기술적으로 기술된 것
- 기계 및 여분의 물품에 대한 별도의 가치(Separately split up value of spares, components, machineries)
- 원산지 증명서(Certificate of Origin), 특혜관세가 적용되는 경우

나. 애로 사례 및 업무상 유의점

□ 통관에 필요한 서류의 기재오류나 서류 상호간 불일치를 수정하기가 매우 어려우며 이로 인해 통관 절차가 2~3주씩 지연되기도 하기 때문에 철저한 서류작성이 필수적임
  ○ S사는 신용장 개설시 'EPS'를 'ESP'로 기재해, 이를 수정해서 통관하는데 3주를 허비함
  ○ 이 경우, 서류상의 오기 수정과 더불어 추가적인 비용이 필요한 경우도 있음

□ 인도 세관은 각 컨테이너별로 내부에 들어 있는 품목의 패킹 리스트와 인보이스목록이 일치하는지를 체크하고, 한 컨테이너 안에서도 박스별로 화물이 일치하는지를 조

사하기 때문에 포장명세서와 인보이스를 철저히 작성해야 함
  ○ 우리나라의 경우는 한 명의 수입상에게 4개의 컨테이너에 해당하는 물품을 수출할 경우 서류를 컨테이너별로 나누지 않고 일괄 작성함

□ 수입업자와 협의하여 통관업체를 지정하는 것이 효율적임
  ○ 우리 측에서 통관업체를 지정하는 경우 대다수가 델리에 본사를 두고 있는 업체임
  ○ 이들은 실질 통관 업무를 각 지방세관의 다른 통관업체에게 재하청을 주는 브로커들인 경우가 많기 때문에 수입업자가 추천하는 통관업체를 지정하는 것이 효율적임

□ 인도 정부는 신용장 방식으로 수입할 경우 보험가입 여부를 철저히 점검하기 때문에 보험가입을 반드시 점검해야 함
  ○ 인도에서는 CIF(Cost, Insurance and Freight, 운임 보험료 포함 인도)조건 수입은 허용되지만 C&F(Cost and Freight, 보험료 제외하고 운임까지 포함 인도)조건 수입시에는 문제가 발생할 소지가 많음

□ 특별관계에 있는 두 회사 간의 수출입은 관세포탈이나 외화도피 가능성이 있다고 여기기 때문에 관계회사 수출을 피해야 함
  ○ 한국의 P사는 인도에 설립한 자회사에 기계 수출시 3%의 추가세를 내게 되어 이의를 제기하고 로비 및 협상을 통하여 당시 1회에 한하여 면제를 받기로 함
  ○ 이를 피하기 위해서는 수출사와 수입사의 이름이 같지 않도록 다른 명의의 무역업체 이름을 사용하여 수출하는 것이 바람직함

□ 인도는 항만·도로 등의 인프라가 낙후돼 있고 운송수단도 노후하기 때문에 내륙운송과정에서 사고가 자주 발생하므로 내륙운송보험에 가입해야 함
  ○ A라는 우리 기업이 대형 발전 프로젝트를 수주하여 터빈 수입시 항구에서 건설부지로 이동 중, 운송차량이 기울어져 설비가 땅에 떨어짐
  ○ B사는 인도주정부가 마련한 공단 부지내 진입로에서 도로포장이 되지 않아 컨테

이너가 전복되어, 기계가 쓰지 못할 만큼 부서짐
  ○ 보험료가 선진국의 3배에 달하지만 운송보험에 가입하는 것이 유리하며, 우리나라보다는 현지에서 가입하는 것이 저렴함

□ HS 코드 분류는 인도 내 수입자와 협의하여 면밀히 검토해야 함
  ○ C라는 우리 투자기업은 제도용 T형 자를 다른 품목과 함께 수입하면서 HS코드를 명확히 검토하지 않아 함께 선적한 다른 품목까지 오랫동안 세관에 묶여, 큰 손해가 발생함
  ○ S사는 스티로폼 원료 수입시 HS코드를 변경함으로써 관세를 절반으로 낮추었음
  ○ T사는 코코아 함유품목의 수입자유화가 발표되자 자사제품의 HS코드를 이 품목에 적용시켜 신규시장개척에 성공함

다. 한-인도 CEPA의 활용

□ 외교통상부 FTA웹사이트(www.fta.go.kr)에서 한-인도 CEPA의 구체적인 협상 내용과 CEPA 관세율을 확인할 수 있음
  ○ 부속서 2-가 "인도의 對한국 양허안"을 살펴보면 HS코드별 CEPA 양허관세를 확인할 수 있으며 또한 자사 품목이 즉시철폐인지, 5년 내 혹은 8년 내 철폐인지 아니면 민감품목이나 제외품목인지 확인할 수 있음
  ○ 인도 관세는 기본관세·부가관세·특별부가관세 등으로 구성되어 있지만, 이 중에서 기본관세만이 CEPA의 양허대상임

□ CEPA 원산지 증명서 발급신청은 관세청에 수출신고를 한 후 또는 선적 후 7일 이내 관세청 FTA포털사이트(fta.customs.go.kr)나 대한상공회의소 무역인증서비스센터(cert.korcham.net/certweb)를 통해 온라인으로 신청할 수 있음

2. 수입신고 및 세관심사 단계

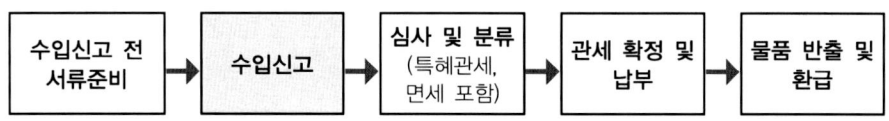

가. 통관 절차상 특이사항

☐ 물품의 가치와 관세의 결정은 관세법 14항(Section 14 of the Customs Act, 1962)에 의해 결정되며, 분류가 명확하지 않거나 자세한 검사가 요청되는 항목에 대해서는 통관신고서 뒷면에 검증된 기관의 검사결과의 평가가 첨부되어야 함

☐ 시험결과 보고서를 통해 세관 검사원은 통관신고서의 최종분류, 물품의 가치와 적용된 관세(기본관세 · 상계관세 · 반덤핑관세 등)에 대해 평가하고, 최종 확인을 위해 세관의 부국장 또는 부청장(Assistant Commissioner/ Deputy Commissioner)에게 제출함

☐ 관세의 평가와 계산 후, 수입 관계자는 재무부 혹은 지정 은행에 관세를 지불한 다음 물품을 반출할 수 있으며, 수입 물품은 이미 물품 분류와 관세 평가가 이루어진 상태이기 때문에 더 이상의 검사나 확인은 필요 없음

☐ 대부분의 경우 세관 검사관이 통관신고서 · 송장 및 관련 서류의 자료를 기초로 평가하며, 수입 물품이 수입이 가능한 물품인지 혹은 제한물품이나 금지물품은 아닌지를 확인한 후에 재검사를 요청할 수 있음

☐ 수입자가 물품의 분류나 관세의 평가에 대해서 만족하지 않을 경우 재심사를 청구할 수 있으며, 검사관의 평가에 대한 항소는 세부규정에 따른 시간과 방법으로 가능함

□ 수입자와 수출자가 특수한 관계를 형성하고 있을 때(예를 들면, 자회사-모회사), 인도에서의 수입자가 SVB Questionnaire를 작성하여 제출해야 함
  ○ SVB(Special Valuation Branch)는 수출자와 수입자의 특수관계가 가격에 영향을 미칠 것을 고려하여 세무당국에서 이를 전담하는 부서임
  ○ 해당 서류를 작성하여 제출할 경우 1%의 Extra Duty Deposit(보증금)을 지불하게 되며, 30일 내에 해당 서류를 작성하여 제출하지 않을 경우 5%까지 Extra Duty Deposit이 상향조정됨

나. 인도 세관 전자자료공유(EDI) 시스템(ICES, Indian Customs EDI System)

□ ICES는 통관신고서를 처리하는 수입 전자자료공유 시스템(ICES/I, India Customs EDI system/Imports)과 선하증권을 처리하는 수출 전자자료공유 시스템(ICES/E, Indian Customs EDI System/Export)으로 구분됨
  ○ 수출입업자, 통관대리인 등은 관련 서류를 전산으로 제출하며, 최종 단계의 물품 검사와 물품의 인도 시기 이외에는 세관에 나올 필요가 없음
  ○ 통관대리인은 원격 EDI 시스템(RES, Remote EDI System)을 이용하여 전산상으로 통관신고서·선하증권 등 관련 서류들을 제출함

□ 통관신고서 평가 EDI 시스템 안에서 화물 신고는 세관 검사관에게 전산상으로 전달되며, 수동 평가 시스템과 같은 방법과 기준으로 평가하지만, EDI 시스템 안에서는 모든 계산이 시스템 안에서 자동적으로 이루어짐

□ 심사 후에 심사를 마친 통관신고서는 세관 서비스 센터에서 출력되며, 추가서류는 물품의 검사 시에 함께 조사되며, 최종 통관신고서는 세관 직원의 최종 관세 지불 확인 후에 출력됨

3. 특혜관세 및 면세의 적용

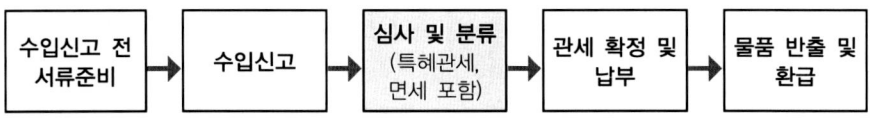

가. 통관 절차상 특이사항

☐ 특별 경제 구역(SEZ, Special Economic Zone) 입주 기업에게는 가장 대표적으로 특별경제구역에 입주 요건(외화 수취액 > 외화 지출액)을 갖추고 입주한 기업에 대해서 자본재나 부품 수입에 대해 관세를 면제해 주고 있음

☐ 수출 촉진용 자본재 관세 감면(EPCG, Export Promotion Capital Goods) 제도에 따르면, 관세 감면을 신청한 제조 또는 수출기업은 자본재 수입시 수입관세를 5%만 납부하면 됨
  ○ 이 자본재를 이용하여 수출품목을 생산해야 하며 관세 감면 금액의 최소 8배에 해당하는 금액을 8년 내에 수출 완료해야 함

☐ 수출목적 자본재 관세 면제(DFIA, Duty Free Import Authorization) 제도는 수출용 원자재의 면세 수입을 가능하게 하는 제도로 수출기업에만 적용됨
  ○ 이 제도는 표준 원재료-완제품 규정(SION, Standard Input and Output Norms)에 따른 품목에만 해당되는 것으로 매우 제한적인 제도임

☐ 서비스 분야 관세 면제 제도는 기존의 서비스분야 관세면제 자격증명(DFEC, Duty Free Entitlement Certificate) 제도를 개선한 것으로, 호텔 및 식당은 식품류 및 주류 수입시 자영 식당업의 경우 20%, 호텔업의 경우 5%의 관세 면제 혜택을 받을 수 있음

□ 수출 유공업체(Status Holder)의 분류를 합리적으로 개선하기 위해 최근 3년간 수출 실적에 따라 5등급으로 구분하여, 우수 수출업자로 선정되는 경우 관세 면제·통관 절차의 신속화·은행보증 면제 등 다양한 혜택이 주어짐

□ 수출전용기업(EOU, Export Oriented Units), 특별경제구역(SEZ, Special Economic Zone) 혹은 소프트 파크(STP, Software Technology Park) 등에 입주한 기업과 인도 국내기업 간의 거래는 수출입거래와 동등하게 취급되어 관세가 부과되나, 외환순수 취 조건 등의 입주조건을 준수하면 수입관세가 면제됨

나. 신용 공인 프로그램(ACP, Accredited Credits Programme)

□ 인도 세관은 AEO(Authorized Economic Operator)제도와 유사한 제도로서 인도 세관의 법과 지침을 준수할 역량과 의지가 증명된 수입업자를 대상으로 신용 공인 프로그램(ACP, Accredited Credits Programme)을 운영 중임
  ○ 이 프로그램은 신용이 공인된 수입업자(Accredited Clients)에게 통관 절차상 편의를 주기 위해 기존의 제도들(EDI와 RMS[17])이 적용되는 기존 체계를 대체하도록 함
  ○ RMS에 의해 무작위로 선택되거나 당국의 지시에 따르지 않는 특정한 패턴이 발견된 경우를 제외하고, 신용 공인 수입업자들은 물품의 검사 없이 수입업자의 자진 심사에 의해 통관을 허락함

□ 신용공인업자에 의해 수입되는 예상 수입화물의 규모에 맞추어 통관시키기 위해 세관은 별도의 시설을 만들 수 있으며, 세관의 국장은 급속한 통관을 위해 별도의 저장공간·처리시설 등을 제공함

---

17) 위험관리시스템(RMS, Risk Management System): 세관의 효율성을 증대시키기 위해 특정한 통관신고서를 기존의 자료를 통해 선별하여 결과를 ICES에 특정 통관신고서 심사와 검사가 필요한지 아니면 관세지불 후 바로 통관이 가능한지 여부를 통보해주는 시스템

□ 위험관리국(RMD, Risk Management Division)은 ACP를 관리하고, RMS에 신용공인 수입업자의 목록을 유지함
  ○ 신용 공인 수입업자들은 세관과 RMD에 의해 모니터링되며, 높은 수준으로 기준을 준수할 것이 요구됨
  ○ 준수 기준이 떨어질 경우 경고가 주어지고, 계속해서 준수하지 않을 경우 ACP 인증 목록에서 제외됨

□ ACP 제도의 오용을 방지하기 위해 신용공인업자들은 통관신고서를 항상 디지털 서명을 사용하여 등록해야 하며, ICEGATE(Indian Customs and Central Excise Electronic Commerce/Electronic Data interchange Gateway)를 통해 통관신고서를 등록하고, 지정된 은행계좌에 관세를 납부해야 함

□ ACP의 신용 공인을 얻기 위해서는 다음의 조건들을 충족해야 함
  ○ 루피화로 평가된 수입물품이 있어야 하고,
  ○ 이전 회계연도에 1억루피 이상의 수입실적과 천만루피 이상의 관세를 지불한 실적이 있어야 하며,
  ○ 개인원장계장에 천만루피 이상의 소비세 납부 실적이 있거나 인도 재무부로부터 수출 유공업체(Status Holder)로 인정되어야 하고,
  ○ 이전 회계연도에 하나 이상의 인도 세관에 적어도 25개 이상의 통관신고서가 등록되어 있어야 하며,
  ○ 이전 3년 이내에 관세·소비세·서비스세에 관한 다음의 경우가 없어야 함
    - 잘못된 신고와 진술·공모·고의 억제·사기 의도를 포함한 관세 회피 사례
    - 압수 물품에 대한 잘못된 신고, 은밀하거나 승인받지 않은 누락 사례
    - 수출촉진제도상의 환불·환급 등의 혜택을 얻기 위한 잘못된 진술과 신고·공모·고의 억제·사기 사례
    - 관세·소비세·서비스세의 납부 지연 사례
    - 관세 및 기타 세금을 회피하기 위한 미등록 사례
  ○ 세관에 의해 실행되는 공동 법령에 기록된 어떤 사례도 없어야 하며,

○ 물품의 분류, 가치 평가, 면세 혜택의 청구 등에 관하여 통관신고서의 내용을 수정한 사실이 이전 년도에 제출된 통관신고서의 20%를 넘지 않아야 하며,
○ 수출의무규정의 불이행에 의해 보류된 관세가 없어야 하며,
○ 신뢰할 만한 기록 보관 및 내부 조정 시스템을 보유해야 하며, 공인 회계기준에 따라야 하고 공인된 회계사로부터 인증을 받은 인증서를 제출해야 함

4. 수입신고 수리 이후 단계

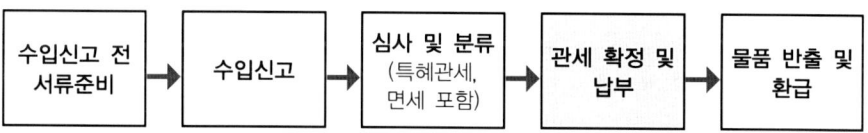

가. 통관 절차상 특이사항

□ 확정된 관세는 지정된 은행에서 지불해야 하고, 지불하기 전에 은행명과 지점명을 확인해야 하며, 은행에서는 세관에 제출할 지불 명세를 공증함

□ 서류 제출 후에 실수를 발견할 때마다 통관신고서의 수정은 부국장의 승인으로 가능하고, 수정에 대한 요청은 증빙서류가 첨부되어야 함
   ○ 예를 들어, 컨테이너 번호를 수정하고자 할 때에는 화물운송회사의 확인서류가 필요함
   ○ 충분한 증거가 부국장에게 제출되었다면, 통관신고서상 내용의 수정은 상품이 통과된 후에 승인됨

나. 애로 사례 및 업무상 유의점

□ 인도 세관에서는 관세 평가 후 관세액을 확정하는데, 관세확정 이후 8일을 초과하면

관세납부 연체료를 연간 20%복리로 부과함
- ○ 관세를 즉시 납부하기 어려운 경우, 관세사를 통해 관세확정을 지연시키면 연체료를 절감할 수 있음

5. 수출 및 환급 단계

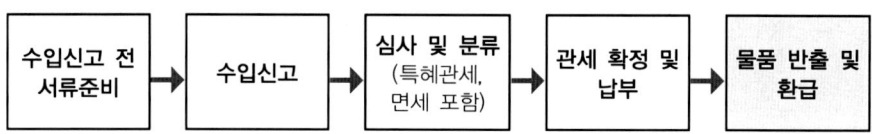

가. 통관 절차상 특이사항

□ 관세환급 제도(Duty Drawback Scheme)에 따르면, 관세 환급법에 의거 운송 서류·수출면장 등을 제출하면 수출품에 관련된 원재료 수입 시 지불한 관세 및 소비세를 환급받을 수 있음
- ○ 환급신청서는 관세소비세 중앙위원회(Central Board of Excise & Customs) 홈페이지(www.cbec.gov.in)에서 받을 수 있으며 신청서를 관세소비세 중앙위원회에 제출한 후 환급에 걸리는 시간은 보통 6개월 정도임

□ 상품의 수출 후에 관세 환급 신청은 EDI 시스템을 통해 자동적으로 이루어지고, 환급 담당 직원에 의해 선착순으로 처리됨
- ○ 선하증권의 상태와 환급요청의 허가는 서비스 센터의 문의에 의해 확인될 수 있으며, 수출업자는 서비스센터의 문의와 부족한 내용에 대해 답해야 함
- ○ 문의와 부족한 내용에 대해 답한 후에야 EDI 시스템상에 등록됨
- ○ 허가된 환급 건에 대해서는 시스템을 통해 은행으로 이전되며, 수출업자의 계좌에 환급내용에 상당하는 금액이 입금됨

나. 애로 사례 및 업무상 유의점

☐ 국제 관례에 의하면 2개월 정도 지나면 항만 측이 내용물을 꺼낸 후 컨테이너는 선사에 반환하는 것이 보통이나 인도에서는 오히려 초과정박 비용(Demurrage Charge)을 컨테이너 소유주에게 부과함
  ○ 컨테이너로 수입한 화주가 나타나지 않아 항만 당국이 컨테이너를 1년 이상 항구에 묶어둔 사례도 있음

참고문헌

대한무역투자진흥공사, 『KOTRA 新 인도 비즈니스 가이드』, 2010.
외교통상부, 『한·인도 CEPA의 주요내용』, 2009.
한국수출입은행, 『인도: 국가현황 및 진출방안』, 2010.
Central Board of Excise & Customs, Ministry of Finance, Government of India, 『Customs Manual 2011』, 2011.
The World Bank Group, 『Doing Business 2011』, 2011.
USTR, 『National Trade Estimate Report on Foreign Trade Barriers』, 2011.
Usha Kiran Rai, 『Export-Import And Logistics Management 2nd ed.』, PHI Learning, New Delhi, 2010.

대한무역투자진흥공사, 국가정보→인도, 주소: http://www.kotra.or.kr
대한민국 관세청, 주소: http://www.customs.go.kr
인도 관세소비세 중앙위원회, 주소: http://www.cbec.gov.in
인도 관세평가국, 주소: http://www.dov.gov.in
인도정부 비즈니스 포탈, 주소: http://business.gov.in
해외진출 정보시스템, 국가정보→인도, 주소: http://www.ois.go.kr

부록 Ⅰ. Business Tip[1]

□ 인도인들은 시간 엄수를 높이 평가하지만 스스로가 실천하지 않는 편이며, 언제든지 약속이 바뀔 가능성이 있다는 것을 염두에 두고 스케줄을 유동성 있게 잡는 것이 좋음

□ 계약 체결과 관련된 의사결정은 오직 최고위층에 의해서만 이루어지며, 중간 관리층에서는 의사결정을 내리지 않지만 어느 정도는 영향력을 갖고 있음

□ 근무시간은 통상 9시 30분에서 5시까지이며, 인도 경영층은 11시에서 4시 사이에 약속을 잡는 것을 선호함

□ 수많은 종교적 휴일에는 비즈니스가 이루어지지 않으며, 지역별로 서로 다른 공휴일들이 있고 해마다 날짜가 바뀌므로 사전에 미리 확인해야 함

□ 스케줄 변경과 지연은 인도 비즈니스의 일부분이며, 인도 가정에서 아이들을 결혼시키고, 관혼상제를 치르고, 일가친척과 양친을 보살피는 것은 남자의 일임을 고려해야 함

□ 남성은 정장과 넥타이를 갖추어야 하고, 더운 날씨에는 넥타이 착용을 생략할 수 있으며, 가죽으로 된 의상·지갑·벨트는 피해야 함

□ 인도인들은 개방적이고 우호적이며 서구국가에 비해 사생활에 대한 관념이 낮은 편이기 때문에 때로는 지나치게 사적인 질문을 하는 경우도 있음

---

1) KOTRA(2010), 'KOTRA 新 인도 비즈니스 가이드' pp.105~110

○ 인도인에게 있어 가족과 개인의 생활에 대해 서로 이야기하는 것은 매우 일반적이며, 심지어 가족에 대해 자주 물어보는 것을 우호의 표시로 해석하기도 함

□ 인도인들은 직접적인 반대표시를 하지 않으므로 드러내놓고 반대의사를 표시하는 것은 적대적인 태도로 인식함

□ 인도인들에게 매우 인기 있는 세 가지 화제는 정치·크리켓·영화이며, 최근에 경제개발에 관한 내용이 추가되었음

□ 인도인들은 자신들의 풍부한 문화유산에 자긍심을 갖고 있으며, 특히 외국인들에게 그들의 역사와 전통에 대해 이야기하는 것을 즐김

□ 종교에 관해서 논하는 것은 가급적 피하는 것이 좋지만 한편으로 종교는 그들의 일상에 매우 깊게 뿌리박고 있기 때문에 특정 종교의식에 대한 순수한 질문은 환영받을 수 있음

□ 대부분의 국민이 파키스탄에 대해서 매우 좋지 않은 감정을 갖고 있기 때문에 이와 관련된 주제는 피하는 것이 좋음

□ 자신들의 경제발전을 매우 자랑스러워하기 때문에 빈곤문제에 대해 이야기하는 것을 매우 꺼리며, 만약 외국인이 먼저 그런 주제를 꺼낸다면 아주 무례한 비판으로 받아들이기 쉬움

□ 인도사람들은 성(surname)을 일반적으로 사용하며 북인도에서는 특히 그러하고, 여성은 남편의 성을 따름

□ 한 사람의 지위는 나이·학력·직업·카스트에 따라 정해지는 경향이 있으며, 특히 정부기관에 근무하는 것은 민간부문에 종사하는 것보다 훨씬 고상한 것으로 인식됨

부록 Ⅱ. 주요 유관 기관 정보

■ 주 인도 대한민국 대사관

웹페이지	http://ind.mofat.go.kr/
이메일	india@mofat.go.kr

대사관

주소	9 Chandragupta Marg, Chanakyapuri Extension, New Delhi - 110021, INDIA
전화번호	+91-11- 4200-7000
팩스번호	+91-11- 2688-4840

영사부

전화번호	여권 등 일반 영사 업무: (+91-11) 4200-7087, (+91) 99536-59597 사건 사고: (+91-11) 4200-7083, (+91) 98736-65972
이메일	(비자) : india_visa@mofat.go.kr (여권) : india_consular@mofat.go.kr (사건사고) : india_probe@mofat.go.kr
팩스번호	+91-11- 2687-8554

■ KOTRA 뉴델리 무역관(KBC)

주소	#2, 12th Floor, DLF Cyber Terraces, Building 5-A , DLF Cyber City Phase-III, Gurgaon - 122002, Haryana, India
전화번호	+91-124 4628-500
팩스번호	+91-124 4628-501
이메일	ktcdelhi@ktcdelhi.net

■ KOTRA 뭄바이 무역관(KBC)	
주소	No. 93, 9th Floor, Maker Chambers VI, Nariman Point, Mumbai 400 021, India
전화번호	+91-22- 6631-8000
팩스번호	+91-22- 6631-8780
이메일	ktcmumbai@kotra.or.kr

■ KOTRA 첸나이 무역관(KBC)	
주소	No. 463, Swami Building (Paravatham Block), Anna Salai, Teynampet, Chennai - 600 018
전화번호	+91-44- 2433-7280
팩스번호	+91-44- 2433-7281
이메일	kotra@chennaiktc.com

■ 인도 상공회의소(Federation of Indian Chambers of Commerce and Industry; FICCI)	
웹페이지	www.ficci.com
주소	FICCI, Federation House, Tansen Marg, New Delhi 110001
전화번호	+91-11- 2373-8760~70
팩스번호	+91-11- 2332-0714, 2372-1504
이메일	ficci@ficci.com

■ 인도 관세소비세 중앙위원회	
웹페이지	www.cbec.gov.in
주소	Directorate of Publicity & Public Relations, Customs & Central Excise, Central Revenues Building, I.P. Estate, New Delhi-110 109
전화번호	+91-11- 2337-9331
팩스번호	+91-11- 2337-0744
이메일	webmaster.cbec@icegate.gov.in

■ 인도 관세평가국

웹페이지	www.dov.gov.in
주소	Directorate General of Valuation, Mumbai, New Custom House Annexe (7th floor), Ballard Estate, Mumbai - 400 038.
전화번호	+91-22- 2270-0075, 2263-4519
팩스번호	+91-22- 2269-2503, 2261-4566, 2263-3083
이메일	directorate.valuation@dov.gov.in

■ 인도 국가 무역정보센터

웹페이지	www.ncti-india.com
주소	NCTI Complex, Pragati Maidan, New Delhi - 110001
전화번호	+91-11- 2337-1948, 50, 53
팩스번호	+91-11- 2337-1979
이메일	ncti@ncti-india.com

부록 Ⅲ. 인도의 수출입 통관 절차
(Procedure for Clearance of Imported and Export Goods)[2]

I. Import:

(a) Bill of Entry – Cargo Declaration:

1. Goods imported in a vessel/aircraft attract customs duty and unless these are not meant for customs clearance at the port/airport of arrival by particular vessel/aircraft and are intended for transit by the same vessel/aircraft or transshipment to another customs station or to any place outside India, detailed customs clearance formalities of the landed goods have to be followed by the importers. In regard to the transit goods, so long as these are mentioned in import report/IGM for transit to any place outside India, Customs allows transit without payment of duty.

    Similarly for goods brought in by particular vessel aircraft for transshipment to another customs station detailed customs clearance formalities at the port/airport of landing are not prescribed and simple transshipment procedure has to be followed by the carrier and the concerned agencies.

    The customs clearance formalities have to be complied with by the importer after arrival of the goods at the other customs station. There could also be cases of transshipment of the goods after unloading to a port outside India. Here also simpler procedure for transshipment has been prescribed by regulations, and no

---

[2] 수입 수출 상품의 통관 절차, 인도 관세소비세 중앙위원회 관세평가국 홈페이지(Directorate General of Valuation, Cental Board of Excise and Customs):
http://www.dov.gov.in/newsite3/clearance_procedure.asp

duty is required to be paid.

(Sections 52 to 56 of the Customs are relevant in this regard.)

2. For other goods, which are offloaded importers, have the option to clear the goods for home consumption after payment of the duties leviable or to clear them for warehousing without immediate discharge of the duties leviable in terms of the warehousing provisions built in the Customs Act. Every importer is required to file in terms of the Section 46 an entry (which is called Bill of entry) for home consumption or warehousing in the form, as prescribed by regulations.

3. If the goods are cleared through the EDI system, no formal Bill of Entry is filed as it is generated in the computer system, but the importer is required to file a cargo declaration having prescribed particulars required for processing of the entry for customs clearance.

4. The Bill of entry, where filed, is to be submitted in a set, different copies meant for different purposes and also given different colour scheme, and on the body of the bill of entry the purpose for which it will be used is generally mentioned in the non-EDI declaration.

5. The importer clearing the goods for domestic consumption has to file bill of entry in four copies; original and duplicate are meant for customs, third copy for the importer and the fourth copy is meant for the bank for making remittances.

6. In the non-EDI system alongwith the bill of entry filed by the importer or his representative the following documents are also generally required: −
   - Signed invoice
   - Packing list

- Bill of Lading or Delivery Order/Airway Bill
- GATT declaration form duly filled in
- Importers/CHA's declaration
- License wherever necessary
- Letter of Credit/Bank Draft/wherever necessary
- Insurance document
- Import license
- Industrial License, if required
- Test report in case of chemicals
- Ad-hoc exemption order
- DEEC Book/DEPB in original
- Catalogue, Technical write-up, Literature in case of machineries, spares or chemicals as may be applicable
- Separately split up value of spares, components machineries
- Certificate of Origin, if preferential rate of duty is claimed
- No Commission declaration

7. While filing the bill of entry and giving various particulars as prescribed therein the correctness of the information given has also to be certified by the importer in the form a declaration at the foot of the bill of entry and any mis-declaration/incorrect declaration has legal consequences, and due precautions should be taken by importer while signing these declarations.

8. Under the EDI system, the importer does not submit documents as such for assessment but submits declarations in electronic format containing all the relevant information to the Service Centre. A signed paper copy of the declaration is taken by the service centre operator for non-repudiability of the declaration. A checklist is generated for verification of data by the importer/CHA. After verification, the data is

submitted to the system by the Service Centre Operator and system then generates a B/E Number, which is endorsed on the printed checklist and returned to the importer/CHA. No original documents are taken at this stage. Original documents are taken at the time of examination. The importer/CHA also need to sign on the final document after Customs clearance.

9. The first stage for processing a bill of entry is what is termed the noting of the bill of entry, vis-à-vis, the IGM filed by the carrier. In the non-EDI system the importer has to get the bill of entry noted in the concerned unit which checks the consignment sought to be cleared having been manifested in the particular vessel and a bill of entry number is generated and indicated on all copies.

After noting the bill of entry gets sent to the appraising section of the Custom House for assessment functions, payment of duty etc. In the EDI system, the Steamer Agents get the manifest filed through EDI or by using the service centre of the Custom House and the noting aspect is checked by the system itself – which also generates bill of entry number.

10. After noting/registration of the Bill of entry, it is forwarded manually or electronically to the concerned Appraising Group in the Custom House dealing with the commodity sought to be cleared. Appraising Wing of the Custom House has a number of Groups dealing with earmarked commodities falling under different Chapter Headings of the Customs Tariff and they take up further scrutiny for assessment, import permissibility etc. angle.

(b) Assessment:

11. The basic function of the assessing officer in the appraising groups is to determine the duty liability taking due note of any exemptions or benefits claimed under

different export promotion schemes. They have also to check whether there are any restrictions or prohibitions on the goods imported and if they require any permission/license/permit etc., and if so whether these are forthcoming. Assessment of duty essentially involves proper classification of the goods imported in the customs tariff having due regard to the rules of interpretations, chapter and sections notes etc., and determining the duty liability. It also involves correct determination of value where the goods are assessable on ad valorem basis.

The assessing officer has to take note of the invoice and other declarations submitted alongwith the bill of entry to support the valuation claim, and adjudge whether the transaction value method and the invoice value claimed for the basis of assessment is acceptable, or value needs to be redetermined having due regard to the provisions of Section 14 and the valuation rules issued thereunder, the case law and various instructions on the subject. He also takes note of the contemporaneous values and other information on valuation available with the Custom House.

12. Where the appraising officer is not very clear about the description of the goods from the document or as some doubts about the proper classification, which may be possible only to determine after detailed examination of the nature of the goods or testing of its samples, he may give an examination order in advance of finalisation of assessment including order for drawing of representative sample. This is done generally on the reverse of the original copy of the bill of entry which is presented by the authorized agent of the importer to the appraising staff posted in the Docks/Air Cargo Complexes where the goods are got examined in the presence of the importer's representative.

13. On receipt of the examination report the appraising officers in the group assesses the bill of entry. He indicates the final classification and valuation in the bill of entry indicating separately the various duties such as basic, countervailing,

anti-dumping, safeguard duties etc. those may be leviable. Thereafter the bill of entry goes to Assistant Commissioner/Deputy Commissioner for confirmation depending upon certain value limits and sent to comptist who calculates the duty amount taking into account the rate of exchange at the relevant date as provided under Section 14 of the Customs Act.

14. After the assessment and calculation of the duty liability the importer's representative has to deposit the duty calculated with the treasury or the nominated banks, whereafter he can go and seek delivery of the goods from the custodians.

15. Where the goods have already been examined for finalization of classification or valuation no further examination/checking by the dock appraising staff is required at the time of giving delivery and the goods can be taken delivery after taking appropriate orders and payment of dues to the custodians, if any.

16. In most cases, the appraising officer assessees the goods on the basis of information and details furnished to the importer in the bill of entry, invoice and other related documents including catalogue, write-up etc. He also determines whether the goods are permissible for import or there are any restriction/prohibition. He may allow payment of duty and delivery of the goods on what is called second check/appraising basis in case there are no restriction/prohibition. In this method, the duties as determined and calculated are paid in the Custom House and appropriate order is given on the reverse of the duplicate copy of the bill of entry and the importer or his agent after paying the duty submits the goods for examination in the import sheds in the docks etc. to the examining staff. If the goods are found to be as declared and no other discrepancies/mis-declarations etc. are detected, the importer or his agent can clear the goods after the shed appraiser gives out of charge order.

17. Wherever the importer is not satisfied with the classification, rate of duty or valuation as may be determined by the appraising officer, he can seek an assessment order. An appeal against the assessment order can be made to appropriate appellate authority within the time limits and in the manner prescribed.

(c) EDI Assessment:

18. In the EDI system of handling of the documents/declarations for taking import clearances as mentioned earlier the cargo declaration is transferred to the assessing officer in the groups electronically.

19. The assessing officer processes the cargo declaration on screen with regard to all the parameters as given above for manual process. However in EDI system, all the calculations are done by the system itself. In addition, the system also supplies useful information for calculation of duty, for example, when a particular exemption notification is accepted, the system itself gives the extent of exemption under that notification and calculates the duty accordingly. Similarly, it automatically applies relevant rate of exchange in force while calculating. Thus no comptist is required in EDI system. If assessing officer needs any clarification from the importer, he may raise a query. The query is printed at the service centre and the party replies to the query through the service centre.

20. After assessment, a copy of the assessed bill of entry is printed in the service centre. Under EDI, documents are normally examined at the time of examination of the goods. Final bill of entry is printed after 'out of charge' is given by the Custom Officer.

21. In EDI system, in certain cases, the facility of system appraisal is available. Under this process, the declaration of importer is taken as correct and the system itself calculates duty which is paid by the importer. In such case, no assessing officer is involved.

22. Also, a facility of tele-enquiry is provided in certain major Customs stations through which the status of documents filed through EDI systems could be ascertained through the telephone. If nay query is raised, the same may be got printed through fax in the office of importer/exporter/CHA.

(d) Examination of Goods:

23. All imported goods are required to be examined for verification of correctness of description given in the bill of entry. However, a part of the consignment is selected on random selection basis and is examined. In case the importer does not have complete information with him at the time of import, he may request for examination of the goods before assessing the duty liability or, if the Customs Appraiser/Assistant Commissioner feels the goods are required to be examined before assessment, the goods are examined prior to assessment. This is called First Appraisement. The importer has to request for first check examination at the time of filing the bill of entry or at data entry stage. The reason for seeking First Appraisement is also required to be given. On original copy of the bill of entry, the Customs Appraiser records the examination order and returns the bill of entry to the importer/CHA with the direction for examination, who is to take it to the import shed for examination of the goods in the shed. Shed Appraiser/Dock examiner examines the goods as per examination order and records his findings. In case group has called for samples, he forwards sealed samples to the group. The importer is to bring back the said bill of entry to the assessing officer for

assessing the duty. Appraiser assesses the bill of entry. It is countersigned by Assistant / Deputy Commissioner if the value is more than Rs. 1 lakh.

24. The goods can also be examined subsequent to assessment and payment of duty. This is called Second Appraisement. Most of the consignments are cleared on second appraisement basis. It is to be noted that whole of the consignment is not examined. Only those packages which are selected on random selection basis are examined in the shed.

25. Under the EDI system, the bill of entry, after assessment by the group or first appraisement, as the case may be, need to be presented at the counter for registration for examination in the import shed. A declaration for correctness of entries and genuineness of the original documents needs to be made at this stage. After registration, the B/E is passed on to the shed Appraiser for examination of the goods. Along-with the B/E, the CHA is to present all the necessary documents. After completing examination of the goods, the Shed Appraiser enters the report in System and transfers first appraisement B/E to the group and gives 'out of charge' in case of already assessed Bs/E. Thereupon, the system prints Bill of Entry and order of clearance (in triplicate). All these copies carry the examination report, order of clearance number and name of Shed Appraiser. The two copies each of B/E and the order are to be returned to the CHA/Importer, after the Appraiser signs them. One copy of the order is attached to the Customs copy of B/E and retained by the Shed Appraiser.

(e) Green Channel facility:

26. Some major importers have been given the green channel clearance facility. It means clearance of goods is done without routine examination of the goods. They

have to make a declaration in the declaration form at the time of filing of bill of entry. The appraisement is done as per normal procedure except that there would be no physical examination of the goods. Only marks and number are to be checked in such cases. However, in rare cases, if there are specific doubts regarding description or quantity of the goods, physical examination may be ordered by the senior officers/investigation wing like SIIB.

(f) Execution of Bonds:

27. Wherever necessary, for availing duty free assessment or concessional assessment under different schemes and notifications, execution of end use bonds with Bank Guarantee or other surety is required to be furnished. These have to be executed in prescribed forms before the assessing Appraiser.

(g) Payment of Duty:

28. The duty can be paid in the designated banks or through TR-6 challans. Different Custom Houses have authorised different banks for payment of duty. It is necessary to check the name of the bank and the branch before depositing the duty. Bank endorses the payment particulars in challan which is submitted to the Customs.

(h) Amendment of Bill of Entry:

29. Whenever mistakes are noticed after submission of documents, amendments to the of entry is carried out with the approval of Deputy/Assistant Commissioner. The request for amendment may be submitted with the supporting documents. For example, if the amendment of container number is required, a letter from shipping

agent is required. Amendment in document may be permitted after the goods have been given out of charge i.e. goods have been cleared on sufficient proof being shown to the Deputy/Assistant Commissioner.

(i) Prior Entry for Bill of Entry:

30. For faster clearance of the goods, provision has been made in section 46 of the Act, to allow filing of bill of entry prior to arrival of goods. This bill of entry is valid if vessel/aircraft carrying the goods arrive within 30 days from the date of presentation of bill of entry.

31. The importer is to file 5 copies of the bill of entry and the fifth copy is called Advance Noting copy. The importer has to declare that the vessel/aircraft is due within 30 days and they have to present the bill of entry for final noting as soon as the IGM is filed. Advance noting is available to all imports except for into bond bill of entry and also during the special period.

(j) Mother Vessel/Feeder vessel:

32. Often in case of goods coming by container ships they are transferred at an intermediate ports (like Ceylon) from mother vessel to smaller vessels called feeder vessels. At the time of filing of advance noting B/E, the importer does not know as to which vessel will finally bring the goods to Indian port. In such cases, the name of mother vessel may be filled in on the basis of the bill of lading. On arrival of the feeder vessel, the bill of entry may be amended to mention names of both mother vessel and feeder vessel Specialised Schemes.

33. The import of goods are made under specialised schemes like DEEC or EOU etc.

The importer in such cases is required to execute bonds with the Customs authorities for fulfillment of conditions of respective notifications. If the importer fails to fulfill the conditions, he has to pay the duty leviable on those goods. The amount of bond would be equal to the amount of duty leviable on the imported goods. The bank guarantee is also required alongwith the bond. However, the amount of bank guarantee depends upon the status of the importer like Super Star Trading House/Trading House etc.

(k) Bill of Entry for Bond/Warehousing:

34. A separate form of bill of entry is used for clearance of goods for warehousing. All documents as required to be attached with a Bill of Entry for home consumption are also required to be filed with bill of entry for warehousing. The bill of entry is assessed in the same manner and duty payable is determined. However, since duty is not required to be paid at the time of warehousing of the goods, the purpose of assessing the goods at this stage is to secure the duty in case the goods do not reach the warehouse. The duty is paid at the time of ex-bond clearance of goods for which an ex-bond bill of entry is filed. The rate of duty applicable to imported goods cleared from a warehouse is the rate in-force on the date on which the goods are actually removed from the warehouse. (References: Bill of Entry (Forms) Regulations, 1976, ATA carnet (Form Bill of Entry and Shipping Bill) Regulations, 1990, Uncleared goods (Bill of entry) regulation, 1972, CBEC Circulars No. 22/97, dated 4/7/1997, 63/97, dated 21/11/1997)

II. Export:

For clearance of export goods, the export or his agents have to undertake the following formalities:

(a) Registration:

35. The exporters have to obtain PAN based Business Identification Number(BIN) from the Directorate General of Foreign Trade prior to filing of shipping bill for clearance of export goods. Under the EDI System, PAN based BIN is received by the Customs System from the DGFT online. The exporters are also required to register authorised foreign exchange dealer code (through which export proceeds are expected to be realised) and open a current account in the designated bank for credit of any drawback incentive.

36. Whenever a new Airline, Shipping Line, Steamer Agent, port or airport comes into operation, they are required to be registered into the Customs System. Whenever, electronic processing of shipping bill etc. is held up on account of non-registration of these entities, the same is to be brought to the notice of Assistant/Deputy Commissioner in-charge of EDI System for registering the new entity in the system.

(b) Registration in the case of export under export promotion schemes:

37. All the exporters intending to export under the export promotion scheme need to get their licences/DEEC book etc. registered at the Customs Station. For such registration, original documents are required.

(c) Processing of Shipping Bill-Non-EDI:

38. Under manual system, shipping bills or, as the case may be, bills of export are required to be filed in format as prescribed in the Shipping Bill and Bill of Export

(Form) regulations, 1991. The bills of export are being used if clearance of export goods is taken at the Land Customs Stations. Different forms of shipping bill/bill of export have been prescribed for export of duty free goods, export of dutiable goods and export under drawback etc.

39. Shipping Bills are required to be filed along with all original documents such as invoice, AR-4, packing list etc. The assessing officer in the Export Department checks the value of the goods, classification under Drawback schedule in case of Drawback Shipping Bills, rate of duty/cess where applicable, exportability of goods under EXIM policy and other laws inforce. The DEEC/DEPB Shipping bills are processed in the DEEC group. In case of DEEC Shipping bills, the assessing officer verifies that the description of the goods declared in the shipping bill and invoice match with the description of the resultant product as given in the DEEC book. If the assessing officer has any doubts regarding value, description of goods, he may call for samples of the goods from the docks. He may also call for any other information required by him for processing of shipping bill. He may assess the shipping bill after visual inspection of the sample or may send it for test and pass the shipping bill provisionally.

40. Once, the shipping bill is passed by the Export Department, the exporter or his agent present the goods to the shed appraiser (export) in docks for examination. The shed appraiser may mark the document to a Custom officer (usually an examiner) for examining the goods. The examination is carried out under the supervision of the shed appraiser (export). If the description and other particulars of the goods are found to be as declared, the shed appraiser gives a 'let export' order, after which the exporter may contact the preventive superintendent for supervising the loading of goods on to the vessel.

41. In case the examining staff in the docks finds some discrepancy in the goods, they may mark the shipping bill back to export department/DEEC group with their observations as well as sample of goods, if needed. The export department re-considers the case and decide whether export can be allowed, or amendment in description, value etc. is required before export and whether any other action is required to be taken under the Customs Act, 1962 for mis-declaration of description of value etc.

(d) Processing of Shipping Bill-EDI:

42. Under EDI System, declarations in prescribed format are to be filed through the Service Centers of Customs. A checklist is generated for verification of data by the exporter/CHA. After verification, the data is submitted to the System by the Service Center operator and the System generates a Shipping Bill Number, which is endorsed on the printed checklist and returned to the exporter/CHA. For export items which are subject to export cess, the TR-6 challans for cess is printed and given by the Service Center to the exporter/CHA immediately after submission of shipping bill. The cess can be paid on the strength of the challan at the designated bank. No copy of shipping bill is made available to exporter/CHA at this stage.

(e) Octroi procedure, Quota Allocation and Other certification for Export Goods:

43. The quota allocation label is required to be pasted on the export invoice. The allocation number of AEPC is to be entered in the system at the time of shipping bill entry. The quota certification of export invoice needs to be submitted to Customs along-with other original documents at the time of examination of the export cargo. For determining the validity date of the quota, the relevant date

needs to be the date on which the full consignment is presented to the Customs for examination and duly recorded in the Computer System. In EDI System at Delhi Air cargo, the quota information is automatically verified from the AEPC/TEXPROCIL system.

44. Since the shipping bill is generated only after the 'let export order' is given by Customs, the exporter may make use of export invoice or such other document as required by the Octroi authorities for the purpose of Octroi exemption.

(f) Arrival of Goods at Docks:

45. The goods brought for the purpose of examination and subsequent 'let export' is allowed entry to the Dock on the strength of the checklist and other declarations filed by the exporter in the Service Center. The Port authorities have to endorse the quantity of goods actually received on the reverse of the Check List.

(g) System Appraisal of Shipping Bills:

46. In many cases the Shipping Bill is processed by the system on the basis of declarations made by the exporters without any human intervention. In other cases where the Shipping Bill is processed on screen by the Customs Officer, he may call for the samples, if required for confirming the declared value or for checking classification under the Drawback Schedule. He may also give any special instructions for examination of goods, if felt necessary.

(h) Status of Shipping Bill:

47. The exporter/CHA can check up with the query counter at the Service Center

whether the Shipping Bill submitted by them in the system has been cleared or not, before the goods are brought into the Docks for examination and export. In case any query is raised, the same is required to be replied through the service center or in case of CHAs having EDI connectivity through their respective terminals. The Customs officer may pass the Shipping Bill after all the queries have been satisfactorily replied to.

(i) Customs Examination of Export Cargo:

48. After the receipt of the goods in the dock, the exporter/CHA may contact the Customs Officer designated for the purpose present the check list with the endorsement of Port Authority and other declarations as aforesaid along with all original documents such as, Invoice and Packing list, AR-4, etc. Customs Officer may verify the quantity of the goods actually received and enter into the system and thereafter mark the Electronic Shipping Bill and also hand over all original documents to the Dock Appraiser of the Dock who may assign a Customs Officer for the examination and intimate the officers' name and the packages to be examined, if any, on the check list and return it to the exporter or his agent.

49. The Customs Officer may inspect/examine the shipment along with the Dock Appraiser. The Customs Officer enters the examination report in the system. He then marks the Electronic Bill along with all original documents and checklist to the Dock Appraiser. If the Dock Appraiser is satisfied that the particulars entered in the system conform to the description given in the original documents and as seen in the physical examination, he may proceed to allow "let export" for the shipment and inform the exporter or his agent.

(j) Variation Between the Declaration & Physical Examination:

50. The check list and the declaration along with all original documents is retained by the Appraiser concerned. In case of any variation between the declaration in the Shipping Bill and physical documents/examination report, the Appraiser may mark the Electronic Shipping Bill to the Assistant Commissioner/Deputy Commissioner of Customs (Exports). He may also forward the physical documents to Assistant Commissioner/Deputy Commissioner of Customs (Exports) and instruct the exporter or his agent to meet the Assistant Commissioner/Deputy Commissioner of Customs (Exports) for settlement of dispute. In case the exporter agrees with the views of the Department, the Shipping Bill needs to be processed accordingly. Where, however, the exporter disputes the view of the Department principles of natural justice is required to be followed before finalisation of the issue.

(k) Stuffing / Loading of Goods in Containers

51. The exporter or his agent should hand over the exporter copy of the shipping bill duly signed by the Appraiser permitting "Let Export" to the steamer agent who may then approach the proper officer (Preventive Officer) for allowing the shipment. In case of container cargo the stuffing of container at Dock is done under Preventive Supervision. Loading of both containerized and bulk cargo is done under Preventive Supervision. The Customs Preventive Superintendent (Docks) may enter the particulars of packages actually stuffed in to the container, the bottle seal number particulars of loading of cargo container on board into the system and endorse these details on the exporter copy of the shipping bill presented to him by the steamer agent. If there is a difference in the quantity/number of packages stuffed in the containers/goods loaded on vessel the Superintendent (Docks) may put a remark on the shipping bill in the system and that shipping bill requires

amendment or changed quantity. Such shipping bill also may not be taken up for the purpose of sanction of Drawback/DEEC logging, till the shipping bill is suitably amended for the changed quantity. The Customs Preventive Officer supervising the loading of container and general cargo in to the vessel may give "Shipped on Board" endorsement on the exporters copy of the shipping bill.

(l) Drawal of Samples:

52. Where the Appraiser Dock (export) orders for samples to be drawn and tested, the Customs Officer may proceed to draw two samples from the consignment and enter the particulars thereof along with details of the testing agency in the ICES/E system. There is no separate register for recording dates of samples drawn. Three copies of the test memo are prepared by the Customs Officer and are signed by the Customs Officer and Appraising Officer on behalf of Customs and the exporter or his agent. The disposals of the three copies of the test memo are as follows: –
    - Original – to be sent along with the sample to the test agency
    - Duplicate – Customs copy to be retained with the 2nd sample
    - Triplicate – Exporter's copy

53. The Assistant Commissioner/Deputy Commissioner if he considers necessary, may also order for sample to be drawn for purpose other than testing such as visual inspection and verification of description, market value inquiry, etc.

(m) Amendments:

54. Any correction/amendments in the checklist generated after filing of declaration can be made at the service center, provided, the documents have not yet been submitted in the system and the shipping bill number has not been generated.

Where corrections are required to be made after the generation of the shipping bill No. or after the goods have been brought into the Export Dock, amendments is carried out in the following manners.

- If the goods have not yet been allowed "let export" amendments may be permitted by the Assistant Commissioner (Exports).
- Where the "Let Export" order has already been given, amendments may be permitted only by the Additional/Joint Commissioner, Custom House, in charge of export section.

55. In both the cases, after the permission for amendments has been granted, the Assistant Commissioner/Deputy Commissioner (Export) may approve the amendments on the system on behalf of the Additional/Joint Commissioner. Where the print out of the Shipping Bill has already been generated, the exporter may first surrender all copies of the shipping bill to the Dock Appraiser for cancellation before amendment is approved on the system.

(n) Export of Goods Under Claim for Drawback:

56. After actual export of the goods, the Drawback claim is processed through EDI system by the officers of Drawback Branch on first come first served basis. There is no need for filing separate drawback claims. The status of the shipping bills and sanction of DBK claim can be ascertained from the query counter set up at the service center. If any query has been raised or deficiency noticed, the same is shown on the terminal. A print out of the query/deficiency may be obtained by the authorized person of the exporter from the service center. The exporters are required to reply to such queries through the service center. The claim will come in queue of the EDI system only after reply to queries/deficiencies are entered by the Service Center.

57. All the claims sanctioned on a particular day are enumerated in a scroll and transferred to the Bank through the system. The bank credits the drawback amount in the respective accounts of the exporters. Bank may send a fortnightly statement to the exporters of such credits made in their accounts.

58. The Steamer Agent/Shipping Line may transfer electronically the EGM to the Customs EDI system so that the physical export of the goods is confirmed, to enable the Customs to sanction the drawback claims.

(o) Generation of Shipping Bills:

59. After the "let export" order is given on the system by the Appraiser, the Shipping Bill is generated by the system in two copies i.e., one Customs copy, one exporter's copy (E.P. copy is generated after submission of EGM). After obtaining the print out the appraiser obtains the signatures of the Customs Officer on the examination report and the representative of the CHA on both copies of the shipping bill and examination report. The Appraiser thereafter signs & stamps both the copies of the shipping bill at the specified place.

60. The Appraiser also signs and stamps the original & duplicate copy of SDF. Customs copy of shipping bill and original copy of the SDF is retained along with the original declarations by the Appraiser and forwarded to Export Department of the Custom House. He may return the exporter copy and the second copy of the SDF to the exporter or his agent.

61. As regards the AEPC quota and other certifications, these are retained along with the shipping bill in the dock after the shipping bill is generated by the system. At the time of examination, apart from checking that the goods are covered by the

quota certifications, the details of the quota entered into the system needs to be checked.

(p) Export General Manifest:

62. All the shipping lines/agents need to furnish the Export General Manifests, Shipping Bill wise, to the Customs electronically within 7 days from the date of sailing of the vessel.

63. Apart from lodging the EGM electronically the shipping lines need to continue to file manual EGMs along with the exporter copy of the shipping bills as per the present practice in the export department. The manual EGMs need to be entered in the register at the Export Department and the Shipping lines may obtain acknowledgements indicating the date and time at which the EGMs were received by the Export Department.

64. The above is the general procedure for export under EDI Systems. However special procedures exist for specified schemes, details of which may be obtained from the Public Notice/Standing Orders issued by the respective Commissionerates.

부록 Ⅳ. 인도 관세법
(THE CUSTOMS TARIFF ACT, 1975)

Ⅰ. THE ACT

An act to consolidate and amend the law relating to customs duties.

Be it enacted by Parliament in the Twenty-sixth Year of the Republic of India as follows: —

1. Short title, extent and commencement

(1) This Act may be called the Customs Tariff Act, 1975.
(2) It extends to the whole of India.
(3) It shall come into force on such date as the Central Government may, by notification in the Official Gazette, appoint.

2. Duties specified in the Schedules to be levied

The rates at which duties of customs shall be levied under the Customs Act, 1962, are specified in the First and Second Schedules,

3. Levy of additional duty equal to excise duty, sales tax, local taxes and other charges

(1) Any article which is imported into India shall, in addition, be liable to a duty

(hereafter in this section referred to as the additional duty) equal to the excise duty for the time being leviable on a like article if produced or manufactured in India and if such excise duty on a like article is leviable at any percentage of its value, the additional duty to which the imported article shall be so liable shall be calculated at that percentage of the value of the imported article:

Provided that in case of any alcoholic liquor for human consumption imported into India, the Central Government may, by notification in the Official Gazette, specify the rate of additional duty having regard to the excise duty for the time being leviable on a like alcoholic liquor produced or manufactured in different States or, if a like alcoholic liquor is not produced or manufactured in any State, then, having regard to the excise duty which would be leviable for the time being in different States on the class or description of alcoholic liquor to which such imported alcoholic liquor belongs.

Explanation. — In this sub-section, the expression "the excise duty for the time being leviable on a like article if produced or manufactured in India" means the excise duty for the time being in force which would be leviable on a like article if produced or manufactured in India or, if a like article is not so produced or manufactured, which would be leviable on the class or description of articles to which the imported article belongs, and where such duty is leviable at different rates, the highest duty.

(2) For the purpose of calculating under subsections (1) and (3), the additional duty on any imported article, where such duty is leviable at any percentage of its value, the value of the imported article shall, notwithstanding anything contained in section 14 of the Customs Act, 1962, be the aggregate of —
  (i) the value of the imported article determined under sub-section (1) of section

14 or the tariff value of such article fixed under sub-section (2) of that section, as the case may be; and

(ii) any duty of customs chargeable on that article under section 12 of the Customs Act, 1962, and any sum chargeable on that article under any law for the time being in force as an addition to, and in the same manner as, a duty of customs, but does not include —

(a) the duty referred to in sub-sections (1), (3) and (5);

(b) the safeguard duty referred to in sections 8B and 8C;

(c) the countervailing duty referred to in section 9; and

(d) the anti-dumping duty referred to in section 9A:

Provided that in case of an article imported into India, —

(a) in relation to which it is required, under the provisions of the Standards of Weights and Measures Act, 1976 or the rules made thereunder or under any other law for the time being in force, to declare on the package thereof the retail sale price of such article; and

(b) where the like article produced or manufactured in India, or in case where such like article is not so produced or manufactured, then, the class or description of articles to which the imported article belongs, is the goods specified by notification in the Official Gazette under sub-section (1) of section 4A of the Central Excise Act, 1944,

the value of the imported article shall be deemed to be the retail sale price declared on the imported article less such amount of abatement, if any, from such retail sale price as the Central Government may, by notification in the Official Gazette, allow in respect of such like article under sub-section (2) of section 4A of the Central Excise Act, 1944.

Provided further that in the case of an article imported into India, where the Central Government has fixed a tariff value for the like article produced or manufactured in India under sub-section (2) of section 3 of the Central Excise Act, 1944, the value of the imported article shall be deemed to be such tariff value.

Explanation.— Where on any imported article more than one retail sale price is declared, the maximum of such retail sale price shall be deemed to be the retail sale price for the purposes of this section.

(3) If the Central Government is satisfied that it is necessary in the public interest to levy on any imported article [whether on such article duty is leviable under subsection (1) or not] such additional duty as would counterbalance the excise duty leviable on any raw materials, components and ingredients of the same nature as, or similar to those, used in the production or manufacture of such article, it may, by notification in the Official Gazette, direct that such imported article shall, in addition, be liable to an additional duty representing such portion of the excise duty leviable on such raw materials, components and ingredients as, in either case, may be determined by rules made by the Central Government in this behalf.

(4) In making any rules for the purposes of subsection (3), the Central Government shall have regard to the average quantum of the excise duty payable on the raw materials, components or ingredients used in the production or manufacture of such like article.

(5) If the Central Government is satisfied that it is necessary in the public interest to levy on any imported article [whether on such article duty is leviable under subsection (1) or, as the case may be, sub-section (3) or not] such additional

duty as would counter-balance the sales tax, value added tax, local tax or any other charges for the time being leviable on a like article on its sale, purchase or transportation in India, it may, by notification in the Official Gazette, direct that such imported article shall, in addition, be liable to an additional duty at a rate not exceeding four percent. of the value of the imported article as specified in that notification.

Explanation.— In this sub-section, the expression "sales tax, value added tax, local tax or any other charges for the time being leviable on a like article on its sale, purchase or transportation in India" means the sales tax, value added tax, local tax or other charges for the time being in force, which would be leviable on a like article if sold, purchased or transported in India or, if a like article is not so sold, purchased or transported, which would be leviable on the class or description of articles to which the imported article belongs, and where such taxes, or, as the case may be, such charges are leviable at different rates, the highest such tax or, as the case may be, such charge.

(6) For the purpose of calculating under sub-section (5), the additional duty on any imported article, the value of the imported article shall, notwithstanding anything contained in sub-section (2), or section 14 of the Customs Act, 1962, be the aggregate of —
   (i) the value of the imported article determined under sub-section (1) of section 14 of the Customs Act, 1962 or the tariff value of such article fixed under sub-section (2) of that section, as the case may be; and
   (ii) any duty of customs chargeable on that article under section 12 of the Customs Act, 1962, and any sum chargeable on that article under any law for the time being in force as an addition to, and in the same manner as, a duty of customs, but does not include —

(a) the duty referred to in sub-section (5);

(b) the safeguard duty referred to in sections 8B and 8C;

(c) the countervailing duty referred to in section 9; and

(d) the anti-dumping duty referred to in section 9A.

(7) The duty chargeable under this section shall be in addition to any other duty imposed under this Act or under any other law for the time being in force.

(8) The provisions of the Customs Act, 1962 and the rules and regulations made thereunder, including those relating to drawbacks, refunds and exemption from duties shall, so far as may be, apply to the duty chargeable under this section as they apply in relation to the duties leviable under that Act.

3A. Special additional duty

(1) Any article which is imported into India shall in addition be liable to a duty (hereinafter referred to in this section as the special additional duty), which shall be levied at a rate to be specified by the Central Government, by notification in the Official Gazette, having regard to the maximum sales tax, local tax or any other charges for the time being leviable on a like article on its sale or purchase in India:

Provided that until such rate is specified by the Central Government, the special additional duty shall be levied and collected at the rate of eight percent of the value of the article imported into India.

Explanation.— In this sub-section, the expression "maximum sales tax, local tax or any other charges for the time being leviable on a like article on its sale or purchase in India" means the maximum sales-tax, local tax, other charges for the time being in force, which shall be leviable on a like article, if sold or purchased in India, or if a like article is not so sold or purchased which shall be leviable on the class or description of articles to which the imported article belongs.

(2) For the purpose of calculating under this section the special additional duty on any imported article, the value of the imported article shall, notwithstanding anything contained in section 14 of the Customs Act, 1962 or section 3 of this Act, be the aggregate of —
  (i) the value of the imported article determined under sub-section (1) of section 14 of the Customs Act, 1962 (52 of 1962) or the tariff value of such article fixed under sub-section (2) of that section, as the case may be;
  (ii) any duty of customs chargeable on that article under section 12 of the Customs Act, 1962 (52 of 1962), and any sum chargeable on that article under any law for the time being in force as an addition to, and in the same manner as, a duty of customs, but not includes —
    (a) the safeguard duty referred to in sections 8B and 8C;
    (b) the countervailing duty referred to in section 9;
    (c) the anti-dumping duty referred to in section 9A;
    (d) the special additional duty referred to in subsection (1); and
  (iii) the additional duty of customs chargeable on that article under section 3 of this Act.

(3) The duty chargeable under this section shall be in addition to any other duty imposed under this Act or under any other law for the time being in force.

(4) The provisions of the Customs Act, 1962 (52 of 1962), and the rules and regulations made thereunder, including those relating to refunds and

exemptions from duties shall, so far as may be, apply to the duty chargeable under this section as they apply in relation to the duties leviable under that Act.

(5) Nothing contained in this section shall apply to any article, which is chargeable to additional duties levied under sub-section (1) of section 3 of the Additional Duties of Excise (Goods of Special Importance) Act, 1957 (58 of 1957).

4. Levy of duty where standard rate and preferential rate are specified

(1) Where in respect of any article a preferential rate of revenue duty is specified in the First Schedule, or is admissible by virtue of a notification under section 25 of the Customs Act, 1962, the duty to be levied and collected shall be at the standard rate, unless the owner of the article claims at the time of importation that it is chargeable with a preferential rate of duty, being the produce or manufacture of such preferential area as is notified under sub-section (3) and the article is determined, in accordance with the rules made under sub-section (2), to be such produce or manufacture.

(2) The Central Government may, by notification in the Official Gazette, make rules for determining if any article is the produce or manufacture of any preferential areas.

(3) For the purposes of this section and the First Schedule, "preferential area" means any country or territory which the Central Government may, by notification in the Official Gazette, declare to be such area.

(4) Notwithstanding anything contained in subsection (1), where the Central Government is satisfied that, in the interests of trade including promotion of

exports, it is necessary to take immediate action for discontinuing the preferential rate, or increasing the preferential rate to a rate not exceeding the standard rate, or decreasing the preferential rate, in respect of an article specified in the First Schedule, the Central Government may, by notification in the Official Gazette, direct an amendment of the said Schedule to be made so as to provide for such discontinuance of, or increase or decrease, as the case may be, in the preferential rate.

(5) Every notification issued under sub-section (3) or sub-section (4) shall, as soon as may be after it is issued, be laid before each House of Parliament.

5. Notifications to be laid before Parliament

(1) Whereunder a trade agreement between the Government of India and the Government of a foreign country or territory, duty at a rate lower than that specified in the First Schedule is to be charged on articles which are the produce or manufacture of such foreign country or territory, the Central Govern- ment may, by notification in the Official Gazette, make rules for determining if any article is the produce or manufacture of such foreign country or territory and for requiring the owner to make a claim at the time of importation, supported by such evidence as may be prescribed in the said rules, for assessment at the appropriate lower rate under such agreement.

(2) If any question arises whether any trade agreement applies to any country or territory, or whether it has ceased to apply to India or any foreign country or territory, it shall be referred to the Central Government for decision and the decision of the Central Government shall be final and shall not be liable to be questioned in any court of law.

6. Power of Central Government to levy protective duties in certain cases

(1) Where the Central Government, upon a recommendation made to it in this behalf by the Tariff Commission established under the Tariff Commission Act, 1951 (50 of 1951), is satisfied that circumstances exist which render it necessary to take immediate action to provide for the protection of the interests of any industry established in India, the Central Government may, by notification in the Official Gazette, impose on any goods imported into India in respect of which the said recommendation is made, a duty of customs of such amount, not exceeding the amount proposed in the said recommendation, as it thinks fit.

(2) Every duty imposed on any goods under sub-section (1) shall, for the purposes of this Act, be deemed to have been specified in the First Schedule as the duty leviable in respect of such goods.

(3) Where a notification has been issued under sub-section (1), the Central Government shall, unless the notification is in the meantime rescinded, have a Bill introduced in Parliament, as soon as may be, but in any case during the next session of Parliament following the date of the issue of the notification to give effect to the proposals in regard to the continuance of a protective duty of customs on the goods to which the notification relates, and the notification shall cease to have effect when such Bill becomes law, whether with or without modifications, but without prejudice to the validity of anything previously done thereunder.

Provided that if the notification under sub-section (1) is issued when Parliament is in session, such a Bill shall be introduced in Parliament during that session:

Provided further that where for any reason a Bill as aforesaid does not become law within six months from the date of its introduction in Parliament, the notification shall cease to have effect on the expiration of the said period of six months, but without prejudice to the validity of anything previously done thereunder.

7. Duration of protective duties and power of Central Government to alter them

(1) When the duty specified in respect of any article in the First Schedule is characterised as protective in Column (5) of that Schedule, that duty shall have effect only up to and inclusive of the date, if any, specified in that Schedule.

(2) Where in respect of any such article the Central Government is satisfied after such inquiry as it thinks necessary that such duty has become ineffective or excessive for the purpose of securing the protection intended to be afforded by it to a similar article manufactured in India and that circumstances exist which render it necessary to take immediate action, it may, by notification in the Official Gazette, increase or reduce such duty to such extent as it thinks necessary.

(3) Every notification under sub-section (2), in so far as it relates to increase of such duty, shall be laid before each House of Parliament if it is sitting as soon as may be after the issue of the notification, and if it is not sitting within seven days of its re-assembly, and the Central Government shall seek the approval of Parliament to the notification by a resolution moved within a period of fifteen days beginning with the day on which the notification is so laid before the House of the People and if Parliament makes any modification in the notification or directs that the notification should cease to have effect, the notification shall

thereafter have effect only in such modified form or be of no effect, as the case may be, but without prejudice to the validity of anything previously done thereunder.

(4) For the removal of doubts, it is hereby declared that any notification issued under sub-section (2), including any such notification approved or modified under sub-section (3), may be rescinded by the Central Government at any time by notification in the Official Gazette.

8. Emergency power of Central Government to increase or levy export duties

(1) Where, in respect of any article, whether included in the Second Schedule or not, the Central Government is satisfied that the export duty leviable thereon should be increased or that an export duty should be levied, and that circumstances exist which render it necessary to take immediate action, the Central Government may, by notification in the Official Gazette, direct an amendment of the Second Schedule to be made so as to provide for an increase in the export duty leviable or, as the case may be, for the levy of an export duty, on that article.

(2) The provisions of sub-sections (3) and (4) of Section 7 shall apply to any notification issued under sub-section (1) as they apply in relation to any notification increasing duty issued under sub-section (2) of Section 7.

8A. Emergency power of Central Government to increase import duties

(1) Where in respect of any article included in the First Schedule, the Central

Government is satisfied that the import duty leviable thereon under section 12 of the Customs Act (52 of 1962), should be increased and that circumstances exist which render it necessary to take immediate action, it may, by notification in the Official Gazette, direct an amendment of that Schedule to be made so as to provide for an increase in the import duty leviable on such article to such extent as it thinks necessary:

Provided that the Central Government shall not issue any notification under this sub-section for substituting the rate of import duty in respect of any article as specified by an earlier notification issued under this sub-section by that Government before such earlier notification has been approved with or without modifications under sub-section (2).

(2) The provisions of sub-sections (3) and (4) of Section 7 shall apply to any notification issued under sub-section (1) as they apply in relation to any notification increasing duty issued under sub-section (2) of Section 7.

8B. Power of Central Government to impose safeguard duty

(1) If the Central Government, after conducting such enquiry as it deems fit, is satisfied that any article is imported into India in such increased quantities and under such conditions so as to cause or threatening to cause serious injury to domestic industry, then, it may, by notification in the Official Gazette, impose a safeguard duty on that article:

Provided that no such duty shall be imposed on an article originating from a developing country so long as the share of imports of that article from that country does not exceed three percent or where the article is originating from more than one developing countries, then, so long as the aggregate of the imports from all such countries taken together does not exceed nine percent of the total imports of that article into India.

Provided further that the Central Government may, by notification in the Official Gazette, except such quantity of any article as it may be specified in the notification, when imported from any country or territory into India, from payment of the whole or part of the safeguard duty leviable thereon.

(2) The Central Government may, pending the determination under sub-section (1) impose a provisional safeguard duty under this sub-section on the basis of a preliminary determination that increased imports have caused or threatened to cause serious injury to a domestic industry:

Provided that where, on final determination, the Central Government is of the opinion that increased imports have not caused or threatened to cause serious injury to a domestic industry, it shall refund the duty so collected:

Provided further that the provisional safeguard duty shall not remain in force for more than two hundred days from the date on which it was imposed.

(2A) Notwithstanding anything contained in subsection (f) and sub-section (2), a notification issued under sub-section (f) or any safeguard duty imposed under subsection (2), unless specifically made applicable in such notification or such imposition, as the case may be, shall not apply to articles imported by a hundred percent. exportoriented undertaking or a unit in a free trade zone or in a special economic zone.

Explanation.— For the purposes of this section, the expressions "hundred percent. export-oriented undertaking", "free trade zone" and "special economic zone" shall have the meanings assigned to them in Explanation 2 to sub-section (f) of section 3 of Central Excise Act, 1944.

(3) The duty chargeable under this section shall be in addition to any other duty imposed under this Act or under any other law for the time being in force.

(4) The duty imposed under this section shall, unless revoked earlier, cause to have effect on the expiry of four years from the date of such imposition:

Provided that if the Central Government is of the opinion that the domestic industry has taken measures to adjust to such injury or threat thereof and it is necessary that the safeguard duty should continue to be imposed, it may extend the period of such imposition:

Provided further that in no case the safeguard duty shall continue to be imposed beyond a period of ten years from the date on which such duty was first imposed.

(4A) The provisions of the Customs Act, 1962 and the rules and regulations made thereunder, including those relating to the date for determination of rate of duty, assessment, non-levy, shortlevy, refunds, interest, appeals, offences and penalties shall, as far as may be, apply to the dutychargeable under this section as they apply in relation to duties leviable under that Act.

(5) The Central Government may, by notification in the Official Gazette, make rules for the purposes of this section, and without prejudice to the generality of the foregoing, such rules may provide for the manner in which articles liable for

safeguard duty may be identified and for the manner in which the causes of serious injury or causes of threat of serious injury in relation to such articles may be determined and for the assessment and collection of such safeguard duty.

(6) For the purposes of this section, −
  (a) "developing country" means a country notified by the Central Government in the Official Gazette for the purposes of this section;
  (b) "domestic industry" means the producers −
    (i) as a whole of the like article or a directly competitive article in India; or
    (ii) whose collective output of the like article or a directly competitive article in India constitutes a major share of the total production of the said article in India;
  (c) "serious injury" means an injury causing significant overall impairment in the position of a domestic industry;
  (d) "threat of serious injury" means a clear and imminent danger of serious injury.

(7) Every notification issued under this section shall, as soon as may be after it is issued, be laid before each House of Parliament.

[Validation of certain actions taken under section 8B of Act 51 of 1975]

Any action taken or anything done or omitted to be done or purported to have been taken or done or omitted to be done under any rule, regulation, notification or order made or issued under the Customs Act, or any notification or order issued under such rule or regulation at any time during the period commencing on and from the 14th day of May, 1997 and ending with the day, the Finance (No. 2) Bill, 2009 receives the assent of the President shall be deemed to be, and to have always been, for all purposes, as validly and effectively taken or done or omitted to be done as if the amendment made in section 8B of the Customs Tariff Act by section 94 of Finance (No. 2) Act, 2009 had been in force at all material times and accordingly, notwithstanding anything contained in any judgment, decree or order of any court, tribunal or other authority, —

(a) any action taken or anything done or omitted to be done, during the said period in respect of any goods, under any such rule, regulation, notification or order, shall be deemed to be and shall be deemed always to have been, as validly taken or done or omitted to be done as if the amendment made by the said section had been in force at all material times;

(b) no suit or other proceedings shall be maintained or continued in any court, tribunal or other authority for any action taken or anything done or omitted to be done, in respect of any goods, under any such rule, regulation, notification or order, and no enforcement shall be made by any court, of any decree or order relating to such action taken or anything done or omitted to be done as if the amendment made by the said section had been in force at all material times;

(c) recovery shall be made of all such amounts of duty or interest or penalty or fine or other charges which have not been collected or, as the case may be, which have been refunded, as if the amendment made by the said section had been in force at all material times.

Explanation.— For the removal of doubts, it is hereby declared that no act or omission on the part of any person shall be punishable as an offence which would not have been so punishable if this section had not come into force.

8C. Power of Central Government to impose transitional product specific safeguard duty on imports from the People's Republic of China[3]

(1) Notwithstanding anything contained in section 8B, if the Central Government, after conducting such enquiry as it deems fit, is satisfied that any article is imported into India, from the People's Republic of China, in such increased quantities and under such conditions so as to cause or threatening to cause market disruption to domestic industry, then, it may, by notification in the Official Gazette, impose a safeguard duty on that article:

Provided that the Central Government may, by notification in the Official Gazette, exempt such quantity of any article as it may specify in the notification, when imported from People's Republic of China into India, from payment of the whole or part of the safeguard duty leviable thereon.

(2) The Central Government may, pending the determination under sub-section (1), impose a provisional safeguard duty under this sub-section on the basis of a preliminary determination that increased imports have caused or threatened to cause market disruption to a domestic industry:

Provided that where, on final determination, the Central Government is of the opinion that increased imports have not caused or threatened to cause market disruption to a domestic industry, it shall refund the duty so collected:

Provided further that the provisional safeguard duty shall not remain in force for more than two hundred days from the date on which it was imposed.

---

[3] Inserted by Sec.123 of the Finance Bill, 2002

(3) Notwithstanding anything contained in subsections (1) and (2), a notification issued under sub-section (1) or any safeguard duty imposed under sub-section (2), unless specifically made applicable in such notification or such imposition, as the case may be, shall not apply to articles imported by a hundred percent. export-oriented undertaking or a unit in a free trade zone or in a special economic zone.

Explanation.— For the purposes of this section, the expressions "hundred percent. export-oriented undertaking", "Free trade zone" and "special economic zone" shall have the meanings respectively assigned to them in Explanation 2 to sub-section (1) of section 3 of the Central Excise Act, 1944.

(4) The duty chargeable under this section shall be in addition to any other duty imposed under this Act or under any other law for the time being in force.

(5) The duty imposed under this section shall, unless revoked earlier, cease to have effect on the expiry of four years from the date of such impositions:

Provided that if the Central Government is of the opinion that such article continues to be imported into India, from People's Republic of China, in such increased quantities so as to cause or threatening to cause market disruption to domestic industry and the safeguard duty should continue to be imposed, it may extend the period of such imposition for a period not beyond the period of ten years from the date on which the safeguard duty was first impose.

(5A) The provisions of the Customs Act, 1962 and the rules and regulations made thereunder, including those relating to the date for determination of rate of duty, assessment, non-levy, short levy, refunds, interest, appeals, offences and penalties shall, as far as may be, apply to the duty chargeable under this section as they apply in relation to duties leviable under that Act.

(6) The Central Government may, by notification in the Official Gazette, make rules for the purposes of this section, and without prejudice to the generality of the foregoing, such rules may provide for the manner in which articles liable for safeguard duty may be identified and for the manner in which the causes of market disruption or causes of threat of market disruption in relation to such articles may be determined and for the assessment and collection of such safeguard duty.

(7) For the purposes of this section, −
  (a) "domestic industry" means the producers −
    (i) as a whole of a like article or a directly competitive article in India; or
    (ii) whose collective output of a like article or a directly competitive article in India constitutes a major share of the total produced of the total production of the said article in India;
  (b) "market disruption" shall be caused whenever imports of a like article or a directly competitive article produced by the domestic industry, increase rapidly, either absolutely or relatively, so as to be a significant cause of material injury, or threat of material injury, to the domestic industry;
  (c) "threat of market disruption" means a clear and imminent danger of market disruption.

(8) Every notification issued under this section shall, as soon as may be after it is issued, be laid before each House of Parliament.

[Validation of certain actions taken under section 8C of Act 51 of 1975]

Any action taken or anything done or omitted to be done or purported to have been taken or done or omitted to be done under any rule, regulation, notification or order made or issued under the Customs Act, or any notification or order issued under such rule or regulation at any time during the period commencing on and from the 11th day of May, 2002 and ending with the day, the Finance (No. 2) Bill, 2009 receives the assent of the President shall be deemed to be, and to have always been, for all purposes, as validly and effectively taken or done or omitted to be done as if the amendment made in section 8C of the Customs Tariff Act by section 96 of the Finance (No. 2) Act, 2009 had been in force at all material times and accordingly, notwithstanding anything contained in any judgment, decree or order of any court, tribunal or other authority, –

(a) any action taken or anything done or omitted to be done, during the said period in respect of any goods, under any such rule, regulation, notification or order, shall be deemed to be and shall be deemed always to have been, as validly taken or done or omitted to be done as if the amendment made by the said section had been in force at all material times;

(b) no suit or other proceedings shall be maintained or continued in any court, tribunal or other authority for any action taken or anything done or omitted to be done, in respect of any goods, under any such rule, regulation, notification or order, and no enforcement shall be made by any court, of any decree or order relating to such action taken or anything done or omitted to be done as if the amendment made by the said section had been in force at all material times;

(c) recovery shall be made of all such amounts of duty or interest or penalty or fine or other charges which have not been collected or, as the case may be, which have been refunded, as if the amendment made by the said section had been in force at all material times.

Explanation.— For the removal of doubts, it is hereby declared that no act or omission on the part of any person shall be punishable as an offence which would not have been so punishable if this section had not come into force.

9. Countervailing duty on subsidized articles[4]

(1) Where any country or territory pays, or bestows, directly or indirectly, any subsidy upon the manufacture or production therein or the exportation therefrom of any article including any subsidy on transportation of such article, then, upon the importation of any such article into India, whether the same is imported directly from the country of manufacture, production or otherwise, and whether it is imported in the same condition as when exported from the country of manufacture or production or has been changed in condition by manufacture, production or otherwise, the Central Government may, by notification in the Official Gazette, impose a counteravailing duty not exceeding the amount of such subsidy.

Explanation.— For the purposes of this section, a "subsidy" shall be deemed to exist if —
  (a) there is financial contribution by a government, or any public body in the exporting or producing country or territory*, that is, where —
    (i) a government practice involves a direct transfer of funds (including grants, loans and equity infusion), or potential direct transfer of funds or liabilities, or both;
    (ii) government revenue that is otherwise due is foregone or not collected

---
[4] Amended by Sec. 61(a) of Finance Bill, 2006

(including fiscal incentives)

(iii) a government provides goods or services other than general infrastructure or purchases goods;

(iv) a government makes payments to a funding mechanism, or entrusts or directs a private body to carry out one or more of the type of functions specified in clauses (i) to (iii) above which would normally be vested in the government and the practice in, no real sense, differs from practices normally followed by governments; or

(b) a government grants or maintains any form of income or price support, which operates directly or indirectly to increase export of any article from, or to reduce import of any article into, its territory, and a benefit is thereby conferred.

(2) The Central Government may, pending the determination in accordance with the provisions of this section and the rules made thereunder of the amount of subsidy, impose a countervailing duty under this subsection not exceeding the amount of such subsidy as provisionally estimated by it and if such countervailing duty exceeds the subsidy as so determined, –

(a) the Central Government shall, having regard to such determination and as soon as may be after such determination, reduce such countervailing duty; and

(b) refund shall be made of so much of such countervailing duty which has been collected as is in excess of the countervailing duty as so reduced.

(3) Subject to any rules made by the Central Government, by notification in the Official Gazette, the countervailing duty under sub-section (1) or sub-section (2) shall not be levied unless it is determined that –

(a) the subsidy relates to export performance;

(b) the subsidy relates to the use of domestic goods over imported goods in the export article; or

(c) the subsidy has been conferred on a limited number of persons engaged in manufacturing, producing or exporting the article unless such a subsidy is for —

  (i) research activities conducted by or on behalf of persons engaged in the manufacture, production or export;

  (ii) assistance to disadvantaged regions within the territory of the exporting country; or

  (iii) assistance to promote adaptation of existing facilities to new environmental requirements.

(4) If the Central Government is of the opinion that the injury to the domestic industry which is difficult to repair, is caused by massive imports in a relatively short period, of the article benefiting from subsidies paid or bestowed and where in order to preclude the recurrence of such injury, it is necessary to levy countervailing duty retrospectively, the Central Government may, by notification in the Official Gazette, levy countervailing duty from a date prior to the date of imposition of countervailing duty under sub-section (2) but not beyond ninety days from the date of notification under that sub-section and notwithstanding any thing contained in any law for the time being in force, such duty shall be payable from the date as specified in the notification issued under this sub-section.

(5) The countervailing duty chargeable under this section shall be in addition to any other duty imposed under this Act or any other law for the time being in force.

(6) The countervailing duty imposed under this section shall, unless revoked earlier, cease to have effect on the expiry of five years from the date of such

imposition.

Provided that if the Central Government, in a review, is of the opinion that the cessation of such duty is likely to lead to continuation or recurrence of subsidization and injury, it may, from time to time, extend the period of such imposition for a further period of five years and such further period shall commence from the date of order of such extension:

Provided further that where a review initiated before the expiry of the aforesaid period of five years has not come to a conclusion before such expiry, the countervailing duty may continue to remain in force pending the outcome of such a review for a further period not exceeding one year.

(7) The amount of any such subsidy as referred to in sub-section (1) or sub-section (2) shall, from time to time, be ascertained and determined by the Central Government, after such inquiry as it may consider necessary and the Central Government may, by notification in the Official Gazette, make rules for the identification of such articles and for the assessment and collection of any countervailing duty imposed upon the importation thereof under this section.

(7A) The provisions of the Customs Act, 1962 and the rules and regulations made thereunder, including those relating to the date for determination of rate of duty, assessment, non-levy, short levy, refunds, interest, appeals, offences and penalties shall, as far as may be, apply to the duty chargeable under this section as they apply in relation to duties leviable under that Act.

(8) Every notification issued under this section shall, as soon as may be after it is issued, be laid before each House of Parliament.

[Validation of certain actions taken under section 8C of Act 51 of 1975]

Any action taken or anything done or omitted to be done or purported to have been taken or done or omitted to be done under any rule, regulation, notification or order made or issued under the Customs Act, or any notification or order issued under such rule or regulation at any time during the period commencing on and from the 11th day of of January, 1995 and ending with the day, the Finance (No. 2) Bill, 2009 receives the assent of the President shall be deemed to be, and to have always been, for all purposes, as validly and effectively taken or done or omitted to be done as if the amendment made in section 9 of the Customs Tariff Act by section 98 of the Finance (No. 2) Act, 2009 had been in force at all material times and accordingly, notwithstanding anything contained in any judgment, decree or order of any court, tribunal or other authority, —

(a) any action taken or anything done or omitted to be done, during the said period in respect of any goods, under any such rule, regulation, notification or order, shall be deemed to be and shall be deemed always to have been, as validly taken or done or omitted to be done as if the amendment made by the said section had been in force at all material times;
(b) no suit or other proceedings shall be maintained or continued in any court, tribunal or other authority for any action taken or anything done or omitted to be done, in respect of any goods, under any such rule, regulation, notification or order, and no enforcement shall be made by any court, of any decree or order relating to such action taken or anything done or omitted to be done as if the amendment made by the said section had been in force at all material times;
(c) recovery shall be made of all such amounts of duty or interest or penalty or fine or other charges which have not been collected or, as the case may be, which have been refunded, as if the amendment made by the said section had been in

force at all material times.

Explanation.— For the removal of doubts, it is hereby declared that no act or omission on the part of any person shall be punishable as an offence which would not have been so punishable if this section had not come into force.

9A. Anti-dumping duty on dumped articles[5)]

(1) Where any article is exported by an exporter or producer from any country or territory (hereafter in this section referred to as the exporting country or territory) to India at less than its normal value, then, upon the importation of such article into India, the Central Government may, by notification in the Official Gazette, impose an anti-dumping duty not exceeding the margin of dumping in relation to such article.

Explanation.— For the purposes of this section, —
   (a) "margin of dumping" in relation to an article, means the difference between its export price and its normal value;
   (b) "export price", in relation to an article, means the price of the article exported from the exporting country or territory and in cases where there is no export price or where the export price is unreliable because of association or a compensatory arrangement between the exporter and the importer or a third party, the export price may be constructed on the basis of the price at which the imported articles are first resold to an independent buyer or if the article is not resold to an independent buyer, or not resold in the condition as imported, on such reasonable basis as may be determined in accordance with the rules made under sub-section (6);

---

5) Amended by Sec 61(b) of Finance bill, 2006

(c) "normal value", in relation to an article, means —

   (i) the comparable price, in the ordinary course of trade, for the like article when destined[6] for consumption in the exporting country or territory as determined in accordance with the rules made under sub-section (6); or

   (ii) when there are no sales of the like article in the ordinary course of trade in the domestic market of the exporting country or territory, or when because of the particular market situation or low volume of the sales in the domestic market of the exporting country or territory, such sales do not permit a proper comparison, the normal value shall be either —

(a) comparable representative price of the like article when exported from the exporting country or territory to an appropriate third country as determined in accordance with the rules made under sub-section (6); or

(b) the cost of production of the said article in the country of origin along with reasonable addition for administrative, selling and general costs, and for profits, as determined in accordance with the rules made under subsection(6):

Provided that in the case of import of the article from a country other than the country of origin and where the article has been merely transhipped through the country of export or such article is not produced in the country of export or there is no comparable price in the country of export, the normal value shall be determined with reference to its price in the country of origin.

(2) The Central Government may, pending the determination in accordance with the provisions of this section and the rules made thereunder of the normal value and the margin of dumping in relation to any article, impose on the importation of such article into India an anti-dumping duty on the basis of a

---

[6] Amended by Sec 61(b) of Finance bill, 2006

provisional estimate of such value and margin and if such anti-dumping duty exceeds the margin as so determined, −

(a) the Central Government shall, having regard to such determination and as soon as may be after such determination, reduce such anti-dumping duty; and

(b) refund shall be made of so much of the antidumping duty which has been collected as is in excess of the anti-dumping duty as so reduced.

(2A) Notwithstanding anything contained in subsection (1) and sub-section (2), a notification issued under sub-section (1) or any anti-dumping duty imposed under subsection (2), unless specifically made applicable in such notification or such imposition, as the case may be, shall not apply to articles imported by a hundred percent. exportoriented undertaking or a unit in a free trade zone or in a special economic zone.

Explanation.− For the purposes of this section, the expressions "hundred percent. export-oriented undertaking", "free trade zone" and "special economic zone" shall have the meanings assigned to them in Explanations 2 to sub-section (f) of section 3 of Central Excise Act, 1944.

(3) If the Central Government, in respect of the dumped article under inquiry, is of the opinion that −

(i) there is a history of dumping which caused injury or that the importer was, or should have been, aware that the exporter practices dumping and that such dumping would cause injury; and

(ii) the injury is caused by massive dumping of an article imported in a relatively short time which in the light of the timing and the volume of imported article dumped and other circumstances is likely to seriously undermine the remedial effect of the antidumping duty liable to be levied, the Central Government may, by notification in the Official Gazette, levy anti-dumping duty retrospectively from a date prior to the date of imposition of anti-dumping duty under sub-section (2) but not beyond ninety days from the date of notification under that sub-section, and notwithstanding any thing contained in any other law for the time being in force, such duty shall be payable at such rate and from such date as may be specified in the notification.

(4) The anti-dumping duty chargeable under this section shall be in addition to any other duty imposed under this Act or under any other law for the time being in force.

(5) The anti-dumping duty imposed under this section shall, unless revoked earlier, cease to have effect on the expiry of five years from the date of such imposition:

Provided that if the Central Government, in a review, is of the opinion that the cessation of such duty is likely to lead to continuation or recurrence of dumping and injury, it may, from time to time, extend the period of such imposition for a further period of five years and such further period shall commence from the date of order of such extension.

Provided further that where a review initiated before the expiry of the aforesaid period of five years has not come to a conclusion before such expiry, the anti-dumping duty may continue to remain in force pending the outcome of such a review for a further period not exceeding one year.

(6) The margin of dumping as referred to in subsection (1) or sub-section (2) shall, from time to time, be ascertained and determined by the Central Government, after such inquiry as it may consider necessary and the Central Government

may, by notification in the Official Gazette, make rules for the purposes of this section, and without prejudice to the generality of the foregoing such rules may provide for the manner in which articles liable for any anti-dumping duty under this section may be identified and for the manner in which the export price and the normal value of and the margin of dumping in relation to, such articles may be determined and for the assessment and collection of such anti-dumping duty.

(6A) The margin of dumping in relation to an article, exported by an exporter or producer, under inquiry under subsection (6) shall be determined on the basis of records concerning normal value and export price maintained, and information provided, by such exporter or producer:

Provided that where an exporter or producer fails to provide such records or information, the margin of dumping for such exporter or producer shall be determined on the basis of facts available.;

(7) Every notification issued under this section shall, as soon as may be after it is issued, be laid before each House of Parliament.

(8) The provisions of the Customs Act, 1962 and the rules and regulations made thereunder, including those relating to the date for determination of rate of duty, assessment, non-levy, short levy, refunds, interest, appeals, offences and penalties shall, as far as may be, apply to the duty chargeable under this section as they apply in relation to duties leviable under that Act.[7]

---

7) Substituted on and from the Ist day of January, 1995

[Validation of certain actions taken under section 9A of Act 51 of 1975]

Any action taken or anything done or omitted to be done or purported to have been taken or done or omitted to be done under any rule, regulation, notification or order made or issued under the Customs Act, or any notification or order issued under such rule or regulation at any time during the period commencing on and from the 1st day of January, 1995 and ending with the day, the Finance (No. 2) Bill, 2009 receives the assent of the President shall be deemed to be, and to have always been, for all purposes, as validly and effectively taken or done or omitted to be done as if the amendment made in section 9A of the Customs Tariff Act by clause (iii) of section 100 of the Finance (No. 2) Act, 2009 had been in force at all material times and accordingly, notwithstanding anything contained in any judgment, decree or order of any court, tribunal or other authority, −

(a) any action taken or anything done or omitted to be done, during the said period in respect of any goods, under any such rule, regulation, notification or order, shall be deemed to be and shall be deemed always to have been, as validly taken or done or omitted to be done as if the amendment made by the said section had been in force at all material times;

(b) no suit or other proceedings shall be maintained or continued in any court, tribunal or other authority for any action taken or anything done or omitted to be done, in respect of any goods, under any such rule, regulation, notification or order, and no enforcement shall be made by any court, of any decree or order relating to such action taken or anything done or omitted to be done a if the amendment made by the said section had been in force at all material times;

(c) recovery shall be made of all such amounts of duty or interest or penalty or fine or other charges which have not been collected or, as the case may be, which have been refunded, as if the amendment made by the said section had been in force at all material times.

Explanation.— For the removal of doubts, it is hereby declared that no act or omission on the part of any person shall be punishable as an offence which would not have been so punishable if this section had not come into force.

9AA. (1) Where an importer proves to the satisfaction of the Central Government that he has paid any anti-dumping duty imposed under sub-section (1) of section 9A on any article, in excess of the actual margin of dumping in relation to such article, he shall be entitled to refund of such excise duty;

Provided that such importer shall not be entitled to refund of so much of such excess duty under this sub-section which is refundable under sub-section (2) of section 9A.

Explanation.— For the purposes of this sub-section, the expressions, "margin of dumping", "export price" and "normal value" shall have the same meaning respectively assigned to them in the Explanation to sub-section (1) of section 9A.

(2) the Central Government may, by notification in the Official Gazette, make rules to—
   (i) provide for the manner in which and the time within which the importer may make application for the purposes of sub-section (1);
   (ii) authorise theofficer of the Central Government who shall dispose of such application on behalf of the Central Government within the time specified in such rules; and

(iii) provide the manner in which the excess duty referred to in sub-section (1) shall be —
  (A) determined by the officer referred to in clause (ii); and
  (B) refunded by the Deputy Commissioner of Customs or Assistant Commissioner of Customs, as the case may be, after such determination;

9B. No levy under section 9 or section 9A in certain cases

(1) Notwithstanding anything contained in section 9 or section 9A, —
  (a) no article shall be subjected to both countervailing duty and anti-dumping duty to compensate for the same situation of dumping or export subsidization;
  (b) the Central Government shall not levy any countervailing duty or anti-dumping duty —
   (i) under section 9 or section 9A by reasons of exemption of such articles from duties or taxes borne by the like article when meant for consumption in the country of origin or exportation or by reasons of refund of such duties or taxes;
   (ii) under sub-section (1) of either of section 9 and section 9A, on the import into India of any article from a member country of the World Trade Organisation or from a country with whom Government of India has a most favoured nation agreement (hereafter referred to as a specified country), unless in accordance with the rules made under sub-section (2) of this section, a determination has been made that import of such article into India causes or threatens material injury to any established industry in India or materially retards the establishment of any industry in India; and
   (iii) under sub-section (2) of either of section 9 and section 9A, on import into India of any article from the specified countries unless in accordance with

the rules made under sub-section (2) of this section, a preliminary findings has been made of subsidy or dumping and consequent injury to domestic industry; and a further determination has also been made that a duty is necessary to prevent injury being caused during the investigation:

Provided that nothing contained in sub-clauses (ii) and (iii) of this clause shall apply if a countervailing duty or an anti-dumping duty has been imposed on any article to prevent injury or threat of an injury to the domestic industry of a third country exporting the like articles to India;

(c) the Central Government may not levy —
  (i) any countervailing duty under section 9, at any time, upon receipt of satisfactory voluntary undertakings from the Government of the exporting country or territory agreeing to eliminate or limit the subsidy or take other measures concerning its effect, or the exporter agreeing to revise the price of the article and if the Central Government is satisfied that the injurious effect of the subsidy is eliminated thereby;
  (ii) any anti-dumping duty under section 9A, at any time, upon receipt of satisfactory voluntary under taking from any exporter to revise its prices or to cease exports to the area in question at dumped price and if the Central Government is satisfied that the injurious effect of dumping is eliminated by such action.

(2) The Central Government may, by notification in the Official Gazette, make rules for the purposes of this section, and without prejudice to the generality of the foregoing, such rules may provide for the manner in which any investigation may be made for the purposes of this section, the factors to which regard shall be had in any such investigation and for all matters connected with such

investigation.

9C. Appeal

(1) An appeal against the order of determination or review thereof regarding the existence, degree and effect of any subsidy or dumping in relation to import of any article shall lie to the Customs, Excise and Gold (Control) Appellate Tribunal constituted under section 129 of the Customs Act, 1962 (52 of 1962) (hereinafter referred to as the Appellate Tribunal).

(1A) An appeal under sub-section (1) shall be accompanied by a fee of fifteen thousand rupees.

(1B) Every application made before the Appellate Tribunal, −
  (a) in an appeal under sub-section (1), for grant of stay or for rectification of mistake or for any other purpose; or
  (b) for restoration of an appeal or an application, shall be accompanied by a fee of five hundred rupees.[8]

(2) Every appeal under this section shall be filed within ninety days of the date of order under appeal:

Provided that the Appellate Tribunal may entertain any appeal after the expiry of the said period of ninety days, if it is satisfied that the appellant was prevented by sufficient cause from filing the appeal in time.

(3) The Appellate Tribunal may, after giving the parties to the appeal, an oppor-

---

[8] Inserted by Section 2 of the Customs Tariff (Amendment) ordinance, 2003 (1 of 2003) w.e.f. 1.2.2003

tunity of being heard, pass such orders thereon as it thinks fit, confirming, modifying or annulling the order appealed against.

(4) The provisions of sub-sections (1), (2), (5) and (6) of section 129C of the Customs Act, 1962 (52 of 1962) shall apply to the Appellate Tribunal in the discharge of its functions under this Act as they apply to it in the discharge of its functions under the Customs Act, 1962 (52 of 1962).

(5) Every appeal under sub-section (1) shall be heard by a Special Bench constituted by the President of the Appellate Tribunal for hearing such appeals and such Bench shall consist of the President and not less than two members and shall include one judicial member and one technical member.

10. Rules to be laid before Parliament

Every rule made under this Act shall be laid, as soon as may be after it is made, before each House of Parliament, while it is in session for a total period of thirty days which may be comprised in one session or in two or more successive sessions, and if before the expiry of the session immediately following the session or the successive sessions aforesaid, both Houses agree in making any modification in the rule, or both Houses agree that the rule should not be made, the rule shall, thereafter, have effect only in such modified form or be of no effect, as the case may be; so, however, that any such modification or annulment shall be without prejudice to the validity of anything previously done under that rule.

11. Power of Central Government to alter duties under certain circumstances

(1) Where the Central Government is satisfied that it is necessary so to do for the purpose of giving effect to any agreement entered into before the commencement of this Act with a foreign Government, it may, by notification in the Official Gazette, increase or reduce the duties referred to in section 2 to such extent as each case may require:

Provided that no notification under this sub-section increasing or reducing the duties as aforesaid shall be issued by the Central Government after the expiration of a period of one year from the commencement of this Act.

(2) Every notification issued under sub-section (1) shall, as soon as may be after it is issued, be laid before each House of Parliament.

11A. Power of Central Government to amend First Schedule[9]

(1) Where the Central Government is satisfied that it is necessary so to do in the public interest, it may, by notification in the Official Gazette, amend the First Schedule:

Provided that such amendment shall not alter or affect in any manner the rates specified in that Schedule in respect of goods at which duties of customs shall be leviable on the goods under the Customs Act, 1962. (52 of 1962)

---

9) Substituted by S.3 of the Customs Tariff (Amendment) Ordinance, 2003 (No.1 of 2003) w.e.f. 1.2.2003

(2) Every Notification issued under sub-section (1) shall be laid, as soon as may be after it is issued, before each House of Parliament, while it is in session, for a total period of thirty days which may be comprised in one session or in two or more successive sessions, and if, before the expiry of the session immediately following the session or the successive sessions aforesaid, both Houses agree in making any modification in the notification or both Houses agree that the notification should not be issued, the notification shall thereafter have effect only in such modified form or be of no effect, as the case may be; so, however, that any such modification or annulment shall be without prejudice to the validity of anything previously done under that notification.

12. Repeal and saving

(1) The Indian Tariff Act, 1934 (32 of 1934), and the Indian Tariff (Amendment) Act, 1949 (1 of 1949), are hereby repealed.

(2) Notwithstanding the repeal of any of the Acts mentioned in sub-section (1), anything done or any action taken (including any notification published and any rules and orders made or deemed to have been made under the provisions of those Acts and in force immediately before the commencement of this Act) shall, in so far as such thing or action is not inconsistent with the provisions of this Act, be deemed to have been done or taken under the provisions of this Act and shall continue in force accordingly until superseded by anything done or any action taken under this Act.

13. Consequential amendment of Act 52 of 1962

In the Customs Act, 1962 (52 of 1962), in sub-section (1) of Section 12 and in sub-section (1) of Section 14, for the words and figures "Indian Tariff Act, 1934", the words and figures "Customs Tariff Act, 1975" shall be substituted.

Surcharge of Customs under the First Schedule to the Customs Tariff Act or in that Schedule vide Finance Bill No.22 of 1999 dated 27.2.99

(1) In the case of goods mentioned in the First Schedule to the Customs Tariff Act, or in that Schedule, as amended from time to time, there shall be levied and collected as surcharge of customs, an amount, equal to ten percent. Of the duty chargeable on such goods calculated at the rate specified in the said First Schedule, read with any notification for the time being in force, issued by the Central Government in relation to the duty so chargeable.

(2) Sub-section (1) shall cease to have effect after the 31st day of March, 2001, and upon such cesser, section 6 of the General Clauses Act, 1897 shall apply as if the said subsection had been repealed by a Central Act.

(3) The surcharge of customs referred to in subsection (1) shall be in addition to any duties of customs chargeable on such goods under the Customs Act or any other law for the time being in force.

(4) The provisions of the Customs Act and the rules and regulations made thereunder including those relating to refunds, drawbacks and exemptions from duties, shall, as far as may be, apply in relation to the levy and collection of surcharge of customs leviable under this section in respect of any goods as they apply in relation to the levy and collection of the duties of customs on such goods under that Act or those rules and regulations, as the case may be.

II. THE GENERAL RULES FOR THE INTERPRETATION OF IMPORT TARIFF

Classification of goods in this Schedule shall be governed by the following principles:

1. The titles of Sections, Chapters and sub-Chapters are provided for ease of reference only; for legal purposes, classification shall be determined according to the terms of the headings and any relative Section or Chapter Notes and provided such headings or Notes do not otherwise require, according to the following provisions:

2. (a). Any reference in a heading to an article shall be taken to include a reference to that article incomplete or unfinished, provided that, as presented, the incomplete or unfinished article has the essential character of the complete or finished article. It shall also be taken to include a reference to that article complete or finished (or falling to be classified as complete or finished by virtue of this rule), presented unassembled or disassembled.

    (b). Any reference in a heading to a material or substance shall be taken to include a reference to mixtures or combinations of that material or substance with other materials or substances. Any reference to goods of a given material or substance shall be taken to include a reference to goods consisting wholly or partly of such material or substance. The classification of goods consisting of more than one material or substance shall be according to the principles of rule 3.

3. When by application of rule 2(b) or for any other reason, goods are, prima facie, classifiable under two or more headings, classification shall be effected as follows:

(a) The heading which provides the most specific description shall be preferred to headings providing a more general description. However, when two or more headings each refer to part only of the materials or substances contained in mixed or composite goods or to part only of the items in a set put up for retail sale, those headings are to be regarded as equally specific in relation to those goods, even if one of them gives a more complete or precise description of the goods.

(b) Mixtures, composite goods consisting of different materials or made up of different components, and goods put up in sets for retail sale, which cannot be classified by reference to (a), shall be classified as if they consisted of the material or component which gives them their essential character, insofar as this criterion is applicable.

(c) When goods cannot be classified by reference to (a) or (b), they shall be classified under the heading which occurs last in numerical order among those which equally merit consideration.

4. Goods which cannot be classified in accordance with the above rules shall be classified under the heading appropriate to the goods to which they are most akin.

5. In addition to the foregoing provisions, the following rules shall apply in respect of the goods referred to therein:

(a) Camera cases, musical instrument cases, gun cases, drawing instrument cases, necklace cases and similar containers, specially shaped or fitted to contain a specific article or set of articles, suitable for long-term use and presented with the articles for which they are intended, shall be classified with such articles when of a kind normally sold therewith. This rule does not, however, apply to containers which give the whole its essential character;

(b) Subject to the provisions of (a) above, packing materials and packing containers presented with the goods therein shall be classified with the goods if they are of a kind normally used for packing such goods. However, this provision does not apply when such packing materials or packing containers are clearly suitable for repetitive use.

6. For legal purposes, the classification of goods in the sub-headings of a heading shall be determined according to the terms of those sub-headings and any related sub-heading Notes and, mutatis mutandis, to the above rules, on the understanding that only sub-headings at the same level are comparable. For the purposes of this rule the relative Section and Chapter Notes also apply, unless the context otherwise requires.

THE GENERAL EXPLANATORY NOTES TO IMPORT TARIFF

1. Where in column (3) of this Schedule, the description of an article or group of articles under a heading is preceded by "–", the said article or group of articles shall be taken to be a sub-classification of the article or group of articles covered by the said heading. Where, however, the description of an article or group of articles is preceded by "– –", the said article or group of articles shall be taken to be a sub-classification of the immediately preceding description of the article or group of articles which has "–".

2. The abbreviation "%" in any column of this Schedule in relation to the rate of duty indicates that duty on the goods to which the entry relates shall be charged on the

basis of the value of the goods as defined in section 14 of the Customs Act, 1962 (52 of 1962), the duty being equal to such percentage of the value as is indicated in that column In any entry, if no rate of duty is shown in column (5), the rate shown under column (4) shall be applicable.

ADDITIONAL NOTES

In this Schedule, −

(1) (a) "heading", in respect of goods, means a description in list of tariff provisions accompanied by a four-digit number and includes all sub-headings of tariff items the first four-digits of which correspond to that number;

 (b) "sub-heading", in respect of goods, means a description in the list of tariff provisions accompanied by a six-digit number and includes all tariff items the first six-digits of which correspond to that number;

 (c) "tariff item" means a description of goods in the list of tariff provisions accompanying eight-digit number and the rate of customs duty;

(2) the list of tariff provisions is divided into Sections, Chapters and Sub-Chapters;

(3) in column (3), the standard unit of quantity is specified for each tariff item to facilitate the collection, comparison and analysis of trade statistics.

COMMENCEMENT OF CUSTOMS TARIFF (AMENDMENT) ORDINANCE, 2003 (1 OF 2003) [Notfn. No. 16/03-Cus. dt. 24.1.2003]

In exercise of the powers conferred by sub-section (1) of section 25 of the Customs Act, 1962 (52 of 1962), the Central Government, being satisfied that it is necessary in the public interest so to do, hereby makes the following amendments in all the notifications issued under the said sub-section and for the time being in force on the date of the commencement of the Customs Tariff (Amendment) Ordinance, 2003 (1 of 2003), namely:—

In each of the said notifications, for any reference to the Chapter, heading or subheading of the First Schedule to the Customs Tariff Act, 1975 (51 of 1975), as the case may be, relating to any goods or class of goods, wherever occurring in the said notification, the corresponding reference to the Chapter, heading or sub-heading, of the First Schedule to the Customs Tariff Act, 1975 (51 of 1975) as amended by the Customs Tariff (Amendment) Ordinance, 2003 (1 of 2003) shall be deemed to have been substituted.

(2) This notification shall come into force on the date of the commencement of the Customs Tariff (Amendment) Ordinance, 2003 (1 of 2003).

Exemption from Additional Duty in excess of excise duty leviable on like goods [Notfn. No. 89/82-Cus. dt. 25.3.1982 as amended by Notfn. No. 130/90]

The Central Government exempts all the goods covered by the First Schedule to the Customs Tariff Act, 1975 (51 of 1975), when imported into India from so much of the additional duty leviable thereon under section 3 of the said Act, as is in excess of the duty of excise for the time being leviable on like goods produced or manufactured in any place outside a free trade zone in India or hundred percent export-oriented undertaking.

Explanation.— For the purpose of this notification, "free trade zone" and "hundred percent exportoriented undertaking" have the same meaning as in Explanation 2 to sub-section (1) of section 3 of the Central Excises and Salt Act, 1944 (1 of 1944).

COMMENCEMENT OF CUSTOMS TARIFF (AMENDMENT) ORDINANCE, 2003 (1 OF 2003) [Notfn. No. 17/03-Cus. dt. 24.1.2003]

In exercise of the powers conferred by section 3A of the Customs Tariff Act, 1975 (51 of 1975), the Central Government, hereby makes the following amendments in all the notifications issued under the said section and for the time being in force on the date of commencement of the Customs Tariff (Amendment) Ordinance, 2003 (1 of 2003), except as respects things done or omitted to be done before such amendments, namely: —

In each of the said notifications, for any reference to the Chapter, heading or subheading of the First Schedule to the Customs Tariff Act, 1975 (51 of 1975), as the case may be, relating to any goods or class of goods, wherever occurring in the said notification, the corresponding reference to the Chapter, heading and sub-heading of the First Schedule to the Customs Tariff Act, 1975 (51 of 1975) as amended by the Customs Tariff (Amendment) Ordinance, 2003 (1 of 2003) shall be deemed to have been substituted.

(2) This notification shall come into force on the date of the commencement of the Customs Tariff (Amendment) Ordinance, 2003 (1 of 2003).

COMMENCEMENT OF CUSTOMS TARIFF (AMENDMENT) ORDINANCE, 2003 (1 OF 2003) [Notfn. No. 18/03-Cus., dt. 24.1.2003]

In exercise of the powers conferred by section 8B of the Customs Tariff Act, 1975 (51 of 1975), the Central Government, hereby makes the following amendments in all the notifications issued under the said section and for the time being in force on the date of commencement of the Customs Tariff (Amendment) Ordinance, 2003 (1 of 2003), except as respects things done or omitted to be done before such amendments, namely:

In each of the said notifications, for any reference to the Chapter, heading or subheading of the First Schedule to the Customs Tariff Act, 1975 (51 of 1975), as the case may be, relating to any goods or class of goods, wherever occurring in the said notification, the corresponding reference to the Chapter, heading and sub-heading of the First Schedule to the Customs Tariff Act, 1975 (51 of 1975) as amended by the Customs Tariff (Amendment) Ordinance, 2003 (1 of 2003) shall be deemed to have been substituted.

(2) This notification shall come into force on the date of the commencement of the Customs Tariff (Amendment) Ordinance, 2003 (1 of 2003).

COMMENCEMENT OF CUSTOMS TARIFF (AMENDMENT) ORDINANCE, 2003 (1 OF 2003) [Notfn. No. 19/03-Cus. dt. 24.1.2003]

In exercise of the powers conferred by section 9A of the Customs Tariff Act, 1975 (51 of 1975), the Central Government, hereby makes the following amendments in all the notifications issued under the said section and for the time being in force on the date of the commencement of the Customs Tariff (Amendment) Ordinance, 2003 (1 of 2003), except as respects things done or omitted to be done before such amendments, namely: –

In each of the said notifications, for any reference to the Chapter, heading or subheading of the First Schedule to the Customs Tariff Act, 1975 (51 of 1975), as the case may be, relating to any goods or class of goods, wherever occurring in the said notification, the corresponding reference to the Chapter, heading and sub-heading of the First Schedule to the Customs Tariff Act, 1975 (51 of 1975) as amended by the Customs Tariff (Amendment) Ordinance, 2003 (1 of 2003) shall be deemed to have been substituted.

(2) This notification shall come into force on the date of the commencement of the Customs Tariff (Amendment) Ordinance, 2003 (1 of 2003).

THE ACCESSORIES (CONDITION) RULES, 1963. [M.F. (D.R.) Notification No. 18-Cus., dated 23rd January, 1963]

In exercise of the powers conferred by section 156 of the Customs Act, 1962 (52 of 1962), the Central Government hereby makes the following rules, namely: —
1. These rules maybe called the Accessories (Condition) Rules, 1963.
2. Accessories of and spare parts and maintenance or repairing implements for, any article, when imported along with that article shall be chargeable at the same rate of duty as that article, if the proper officer is satisfied that in the ordinary course of trade: —
    (i) such accessories parts and implements are compulsorily supplied along with that article; and
    (ii) no separate charge is made for such supply, their price being included in the price of the article.

Ⅲ. NATIONAL CALAMITY CONTINGENT DUTY (NCCD)

(1) In case of goods specified in the Seventh Schedule to the Finance Act, 2001 (14 of

2001) as amended by the Thirteenth Schedule, being goods imported into India, there shall be levied and collected for the purposes of the Union, by surcharge, a duty of customs, to be called the National calamity Contingent Duty of Customs (hereinafter referred to as the National Calamity Duty of Customs), at the rate specified in the said Seventh Schedule, as amended by the Thirteenth Schedule.

(2) The National Calamity Duty of Customs chargeable on the goods specified in the Seventh Schedule to the Finance Act, 2001 (14 of 2001) as amended by the Thirteenth Schedule shall be in addition to any other duties of customs chargeable on such goods under the Customs Act or any other law for the time being in force.

(3) For the purposes of calculating the National Calamity Duty of Customs under this section on any goods specified in the Seventh Schedule to the Finance Act, 2001 (14 of 2001) as amended by the Thirteenth Schedule, where such duty is leviable at any percentage of its value, the value of such goods shall be calculated in the same manner as the value of article for the purposes of additional duty is calculated under the provisions of sub-section (2) of section 3 of the Customs Tariff Act.

(4) The provisions of the Customs Act and the rules and regulations made thereunder, including those relating to refunds and exemptions from duties and imposition of penalty, shall, as far as may be, apply in relation to the levy and collection of the National Calamity Duty of Customs leviable under this section in respect of the goods specified in the Seventh Schedule to the Finance Act, 2001 (14 of 2001) as amended by the Thirteenth Schedule, as they apply in relation to the levy and collection of the duties of customs on such goods under that Act, or those rules and regulations, as the case may be.

Explanation.– For the removal of doubts, it is hereby declared that for the purposes of this section, on the expiry of the period of operation of the amendments made in the Seventh Schedule to the Finance Act, 2001 (14 of 2001) in terms of section 169, the said Seventh Schedule but for such amendment shall continue to operate as if the said amendment had not taken place.

THE SEVENTH SCHEDULE NOTES

1. In this Schedule, "heading", "sub-heading" and "Chapter" means respectively a heading, sub-heading and Chapter in the First Schedule to the Central Excise Tariff Act.

2. The rules for the interpretation of the First Schedule to the Central Excise Tariff Act, the Section and Chapter Notes and the General Explanatory Notes of the First Schedule shall apply to the interpretation of this Schedule.

Exemption to all goods falling under sub-heading 8517 12 of the Customs Tariff Act [Notifn. No. 26/08-Cus., dt.1.3.2008]

In exercise of the powers conferred by sub-section (1) of section 25 of the Customs Act, 1962 (52 of 1962), the Central Government, on being satisfied that it is necessary in the public interest so to do, hereby exempts all goods falling under sub-heading 8517 12 of the Customs Tariff Act, 1975 (51 of 1975), as specified in column (2) of the Table in the Seventh Schedule to the Finance Act, 2001 (14 of 2001), as amended from time to time, when imported into India, from the whole of the National Calamity Contingent duty of Customs leviable thereon under section 134 of the Finance Act, 2003 (32 of 2003).

Exemption to goods from National Calamity Contingent Duty [Notifn. No. 29/08-Cus., dt.1.3.2008]

In exercise of the powers conferred by sub-section (1) of section 25 of the Customs Act, 1962 (52 of 1962), the Central Government, on being satisfied that it is necessary in the public interest so to do, and in supersession of the notification of the Government of India in the Ministry of Finance (Department of Revenue) No.77/2003-Customs, dated the 14 th May, 2003 published in the Gazette of India, Extraordinary vide number G.S.R. 414(E) of the same date, except as respects things done or omitted to be done before such supersession, hereby exempts all goods (except goods falling under sub-heading 8517 12), as specified in column (2) of the Table in the Seventh Schedule to the Finance Act, 2001 (14 of 2001), as amended from time to time, when imported into India, from so much of the additional duty leviable thereon under sub-section (1) of section 3 of the Customs Tariff Act, 1975 (51 of 1975) as is equivalent to the National Calamity Contingent duty leviable thereon under section 136 of the said Finance Act, 2001.

IV. EDUCATION CESS

Section 91:

(1) Without prejudice to the provisions of sub-section (11) of section 2, there shall be levied and collected, in accordance with the provisions of this Chapter as surcharge for purposes of the Union, a cess to be called the Education Cess, to fulfil the commitment of the Government to provide and finance universalised quality basic education.

(2) The Central Government may, after due appropriation made by Parliament by law

in this behalf, utilise, such sums of the money of the Education Cess levied under subsection (11) of section 2 and this Chapter for the purposes specified in sub-section (1), as if may consider necessary.

Section 92:

The words and expressions used in this Chapter and defined in the Central Excise Act, 1944, the Customs Act, 1962 or Chapter V of the Finance Act, 1994, shall have the meanings respectively assigned to them in those Acts or Chapter, as the case may be.

Section 94:

(1) The Education Cess levied under section 91, in the case of goods specified in the First Schedule to the Customs Tariff Act, 1975, being goods imported into India, shall be a duty of customs (in this section referred to as the Education Cess on imported goods), at the rate of two percent, calculated on the aggregate of duties of customs which are levied and collected by the Central Government in the Ministry of Finance (Department of Revenue), under section 12 of the Customs Act, 1962 and any sum chargeable on such goods under any other law for the time being in force, as an addition to, and in the same manner as, a duty of customs, but not including —
  (a) the safeguard duty referred to in sections 8B and 8C of the Customs Tariff Act, 1975;
  (b) the countervailing duty referred to in section 9 of the Customs Tariff Act, 1975;
  (c) the anti-dumping duty referred to in section 9A of the Customs Tariff Act, 1975; and
  (d) the Education Cess on imported goods

(2) The Education Cess on imported goods shall be in addition to any other duties of customs chargeable on such goods, under the Customs Act, 1962 or any other law for the time being in force.

(3) The provisions of the Customs Act, 1962 and the rules and regulations made thereunder, including those relating to refunds and exemptions from duties and imposition of penalty shall, as far as may be, apply in relation to the levy and collection of the Education Cess on imported goods as they apply in relation to the levy and collection of the duties of customs on such goods under the Customs Act, 1962 or the rules or the regulations, as the case may be.

[Note:— For exemption from Education Cess on specified goods, please see— General Exemption No. 128]

Exemption to specified goods from Secondary and Higher Education Cess [Notifn. No. 28/07-Cus., dt.1.3.2007 as amended by 69/07]

In exercise of the powers conferred by sub-section (1) of section 25 of the Customs Act, 1962 (52 of 1962), read with section 136 read with section 139 of the Finance Act, 2007 (22 of 2007), the Central Government, being satisfied that it is necessary in the public interest so to do, hereby exempts all goods covered under notification of the Government of India in the Ministry of Finance (Department of Revenue), No. 69/2004-Customs, dated 9th July 2004 which was published in the Gazette of India, Extraordinary vide number G.S.R. 411(E), of the same date, from the whole of the Secondary and Higher Education Cess leviable thereon under the said section 136 read with section 139 of the said Finance Act.

V. ADDITIONAL DUTY OF CUSTOMS TO COUNTERVAIL LOCAL TAXES [Notfn. No. 19/06-Cus., dt. 1.3.2006]

In exercise of the powers conferred by sub-section (5) of section 3 of the Customs Tariff Act, 1975 (51 of 1975), the Central Government, on being satisfied that it is necessary in the public interest so to do, and in supersession of the notification of the Government of India in the Ministry of Finance (Department of Revenue), No. 19/2005-Customs, dated the 1st March, 2005[number G.S.R. 117(E), dated the 1st March, 2005], hereby directs that all goods specified under the Chapter, heading, sub-heading or tariff item of the First Schedule to the said Act, having regard to the sales tax, value added tax, local tax and other taxes or charges leviable on sale or purchase or transportation of like goods in India, when imported into India, shall be liable to an additional duty or customs at the rate of four percent ad valorem.

VI. Notification related to Finance Act, 2003: [Notfn. No. 10/06-Cus., dt. 1.3.2006]

In exercise of the powers conferred by section 133 of the Finance Act, 2003 (32 of 2003), the Central Government, on being satisfied that it is necessary in the public interest so to do, hereby appoints the 1st day of March, 2006, as the date on which the provisions contained in the said section of the aforesaid Act shall come into force.

부록 V. 인도 세관법(통관관련 부분)
(THE CUSTOMS ACT, 1962)

CHAPTER V LEVY OF, AND EXEMPTION FROM, CUSTOMS DUTIES

SECTION 12. Dutiable goods

(1) Except as otherwise provided in this Act, or any other law for the time being in force, duties of customs shall be levied at such rates as may be specified under the Customs Tariff Act, 1975 (51 of 1975), or any other law for the time being in force, on goods imported into, or exported from, India.

(2) The provisions of sub-section (1) shall apply in respect of all goods belonging to Government as they apply in respect of goods not belonging to Government.

SECTION 13. Duty on pilfered goods

If any imported goods are pilfered after the unloading thereof and before the proper officer has made an order for clearance for home consumption or deposit in a warehouse, the importer shall not be liable to pay the duty leviable on such goods except where such goods are restored to the importer after pilferage.

SECTION 14. Valuation of goods

(1) For the purposes of the Customs Tariff Act, 1975 (51 of 1975), or any other law for the time being in force, the value of the imported goods and export goods shall be the transaction value of such goods, that is to say, the price actually paid or payable for the goods when sold for export to India for delivery at the time and place of importation, or as the case may be, for export from India for delivery at the time and place of exportation, where the buyer and seller of the goods are not related and price is the sole consideration for the sale subject to such other conditions as may be specified in the rules made in this behalf:

Provided that such transaction value in the case of imported goods shall include, in addition to the price as aforesaid, any amount paid or payable for costs and services, including commissions and brokerage, engineering, design work, royalties and licence fees, costs of transportation to the place of importation, insurance, loading, unloading and handling charges to the extent and in the manner specified in the rules Made in this behalf:

Provided further that the rules made in this behalf may provide for, —
(i) the circumstances in which the buyer and the seller shall be deemed to be related;
(ii) the manner of determination of value in respect of goods when there is no sale, or the buyer and the seller are related, or price is not the sole consideration for the sale or in any other case;
(iii) the manner of acceptance or rejection of value declared by the importer or exporter, as the case may be, where the proper officer has reason to doubt the truth or accuracy of such value, and determination of value for the purposes of this section:

Provided also that such price shall be calculated with reference to the rate of exchange as in force on the date on which a bill of entry is presented under section 46, or a shipping bill of export, as the case may be, is presented under section 50.

(2) Notwithstanding anything contained in sub-section (1), if the Board is satisfied that it is necessary or expedient so to do, it may, by notification in the Official Gazette, fix tariff values for any class of imported goods or export goods, having regard to the trend of value of such or like goods, and where any such tariff values are fixed, the duty shall be chargeable with reference to such tariff value.

Explanation.– For the purposes of this section –
(a) "rate of exchange" means the rate of exchange –
   (i) determined by the Board, or
   (ii) ascertained in such manner as the Board may direct, for the conversion of Indian currency into foreign currency or foreign currency into Indian currency;
(b) "foreign currency" and "Indian currency" have the meanings respectively assigned to them in clause (m) and clause (q) of section 2 of the Foreign Exchange Management Act, 1999 (42 of 1999).

SECTION 15. Date for determination of rate of duty and tariff valuation of imported goods

(1) The rate of duty and tariff valuation, if any, applicable to any imported goods, shall be the rate and valuation in force, –
   (a) in the case of goods entered for home consumption under section 46, on the date on which a bill of entry in respect of such goods is presented under that section;
   (b) in the case of goods cleared from a warehouse under section 68, on the date on

which a bill of entry for home consumption in respect of such goods is presented under that section;

(c) in the case of any other goods, on the date of payment of duty : Provided that if a bill of entry has been presented before the date of entry inwards of the vessel or the arrival of the aircraft by which the goods are imported, the bill of entry shall be deemed to have been presented on the date of such entry inwards or the arrival, as the case may be.

(2) The provisions of this section shall not apply to baggage and goods imported by post.

SECTION 16. Date for determination of rate of duty and tariff valuation of export goods

(1) The rate of duty and tariff valuation, if any, applicable to any export goods, shall be the rate and valuation in force, −
  (a) in the case of goods entered for export under section 50, on the date on which the proper officer makes an order permitting clearance and loading of the goods for exportation under section 51;
  (b) in the case of any other goods, on the date of payment of duty.

(2) The provisions of this section shall not apply to baggage and goods exported by post.

SECTION 17. Assessment of duty

(1) An importer entering any imported goods under section 46, or an exporter entering any export goods under section 50, shall, save as otherwise provided in section 85,

selfassess the duty, if any, leviable on such goods.

(2) The proper officer may verify the self-assessment of such goods and for this purpose, examine ortest any imported goods or export goods or such part thereof as may be necessary.

(3) For verification of self-assessment under sub-section (2), the proper officer may require the importer, exporter or any other person to produce any contract, broker's note, insurance policy, catalogue or other document, whereby the duty leviable on the imported goods or export goods, as the case may be, can be ascertained, and to furnish any information required for such ascertainment which is in his power to produce or furnish, and thereupon, the importer, exporter or such other person shall produce such document or furnish such information.

(4) Where it is found on verification, examination or testing of the goods or otherwise that the self-assessment is not done correctly, the proper officer may, without prejudice to any other action which may be taken under this Act, re-assess the duty leviable on such goods.

(5) Where any re-assessment done under sub-section (4) is contrary to the self-assessment 25 done by the importer or exporter regarding valuation of goods, classification, exemption or concessions of duty availed consequent to any notification issued therefor under this Act and in cases other than those where the importer or exporter, as the case may be, confirms his acceptance of the said re-assessment in writing, the proper officer shall pass a speaking order on the re-assessment, within fifteen days from the date of re-assessment of the bill of entry or the shipping bill, as the case may be.

(6) Where re-assessment has not been done or a speaking order has not been passed on re-assessment, the proper officer may audit the assessment of duty of the imported goods or export goods at his office or at the premises of the importer or exporter, as may be expedient, in such manner as may be prescribed.

Explanation.— For the removal of doubts, it is hereby declared that in cases where an importer has entered any imported goods under section 46 or an exporter has entered any export goods under section 50 before the date on which the Finance Bill, 2011 receives the assent of the President, such imported goods or export goods shall continue to be governed by the provisions of section 17 as it stood immediately before the date on which such assent is received."

SECTION 18. Provisional assessment of duty

(1) Notwithstanding anything contained in this Act but without prejudice to the provisions of section 46,—
  (a) where the importer or exporter is unable to make self-assessment under sub-section (1) of section 17 and makes a request in writing to the proper officer for assessment; or
  (b) where the proper officer deems it necessary to subject any imported goods or export goods to any chemical or other test; or
  (c) where the importer or exporter has produced all the necessary documents and furnishedfull information but the proper officer deems it necessary to make further enquiry; or
  (d) where necessary documents have not been produced or information has not been furnished and the proper officer deems it necessary to make further enquiry, the proper officer may direct that the duty leviable on such goods be assessed provisionally if the importer or the exporter, as the case may be,

furnishes such security as the proper officer deems fit for the payment of the deficiency, if any, between the duty as may be finally assessed and the duty provisionally assessed.

(2) When the duty leviable on such goods is assessed finally or reassessed by the proper officer in accordance with the provisions of this Act, then —
   (a) in the case of goods cleared for home consumption or exportation, the amount paid shall be adjusted against the duty finally assessed and if the amount so paid falls short of, or is in excess of the duty finally assessed, the importer or the exporter of the goods shall pay the deficiency or be entitled to a refund, as the case may be;
   (b) in the case of warehoused goods, the proper officer may, where the duty finally assessed or re-assessed, as the case may be, is in excess of the duty provisionally assessed, require the importer to execute a bond, binding himself in a sum equal to twice the amount of the excess duty.

(3) The importer or exporter shall be liable to pay interest, on any amount payable to the Central Government, consequent to the final assessment order or re-assessment order under sub-section (2), at the rate fixed by the Central Government under section 28AB from the first day of the month in which the duty is provisionally assessed till the date of payment thereof.

(4) Subject the sub-section (5), if any refundable amount referred to in clause (a) of sub-section (2) is not refunded under that sub-section within three months from the date of assessment of duty finally or reassessment of duty, as the case may be, there shall be paid an interest on such un-refunded amount at such rate fixed by the Central Government under section 27A till the date of refund of such amount.

(5) The amount of duty refundable under sub-section (2) and the interest under sub-section (4), if any, shall, instead of being credited to the Fund, be paid to the importer or the exporter, as the case may be, if such amount is relatable to.
   (a) the duty and interest, if any, paid on such duty paid by the importer, or the exporter, as the case may be, if he had not passed on the incidence of such duty and interest, if any, paid on such duty to any other person;
   (b) the duty and interest, if any, paid on such duty on imports made by an individual for his personal use;
   (c) the duty and interest, if any, paid on such duty borne by the buyer, if he had not passed on the incidence of such duty and interest, if any, paid on such duty to any other person;
   (d) the export duty as specified in section 26;
   (e) drawback of duty payable under sections 74 and 75.

SECTION 19. Determination of duty where goods consist of articles liable to different rates of duty

Except as otherwise provided in any law for the time being in force, where goods consist of a set of articles, duty shall be calculated as follows: —
(a) articles liable to duty with reference to quantity shall be chargeable to that duty;
(b) articles liable to duty with reference to value shall, if they are liable to duty at the same rate, be chargeable to duty at that rate, and if they are liable to duty at different rates, be chargeable to duty at the highest of such rates;
(c) articles not liable to duty shall be chargeable to duty at the rate at which articles liable to duty with reference to value are liable under clause (b) :

Provided that, —
(a) accessories of, and spare parts or maintenance and repairing implements for, any

article which satisfy the conditions specified in the rules made in this behalf shall be chargeable at the same rate of duty as that article;
(b) if the importer produces evidence to the satisfaction of the proper officer or the evidence is available regarding the value of any of the articles liable to different rates of duty, such article shall be chargeable to duty separately at the rate applicable to it.

SECTION 20. Re-importation of goods

If goods are imported into India after exportation therefrom, such goods shall be liable to duty and be subject to all the conditions and restrictions, if any, to which goods of the like kind and value are liable or subject, on the importation thereof.

SECTION 21. Goods derelict, wreck, etc.

All goods, derelict, jetsam, flotsam and wreck brought or coming into India, shall be dealt with as if they were imported into India, unless it be shown to the satisfaction of the proper officer that they are entitled to be admitted duty-free under this Act.

SECTION 22. Abatement of duty on damaged or deteriorated goods

(1) Where it is shown to the satisfaction of the Assistant Commissioner of Customs or Deputy Commissioner of Customs —
  (a) that any imported goods had been damaged or had deteriorated at any time before or during the unloading of the goods in India; or
  (b) that any imported goods, other than warehoused goods, had been damaged at any time after the unloading thereof in India but before their examination under section 17, on account of any accident not due to any wilful act, negligence or

default of the importer, his employee or agent; or

(c) that any warehoused goods had been damaged at any time before clearance for home consumption on account of any accident not due to any wilful act, negligence or default of the owner, his employee oragent, such goods shall be chargeable to duty in accordance with the provisions of sub-section (2).

(2) The duty to be charged on the goods referred to in sub-section (1) shall bear the same proportion to the duty chargeable on the goods before the damage or deterioration which the value of the damaged or deteriorated goods bears to the value of the goods before the damage or deterioration.

(3) For the purposes of this section, the value of damaged or deteriorated goods may be ascertained by either of the following methods at the option of the owner: —
 (a) the value of such goods may be ascertained by the proper officer, or
 (b) such goods may be sold by the proper officer by public auction or by tender, or with the consent of the owner in any other manner, and the gross sale proceeds shall be deemed to be the value of such goods.

SECTION 23. Remission of duty on lost, destroyed or abandoned goods

(1) Without prejudice to the provisions of section 13, where it is shown to the satisfaction of the Assistant Commissioner of Customs or Deputy Commissioner of Customs that any imported goods have been lost (otherwise than as a result of pilferage) or destroyed, at any time before clearance for home consumption, the Assistant Commissioner of Customs or Deputy Commissioner of Customs shall remit the duty on such goods.

(2) The owner of any imported goods may, at any time before an order for clearance

of goods for home consumption under section 47 or an order for permitting the deposit of goods in a warehouse under section 60 has been made, relinquish his title to the goods and thereupon he shall not be liable to pay the duty thereon.

Provided that the owner of any such imported goods shall not be allowed to relinquish his title to such goods regarding which an offence appears to have been committed under this Act or any other law for the time being in force.

SECTION 24. Power to make rules for denaturing or mutilation of goods

The Central Government may make rules for permitting at the request of the owner the denaturing or mutilation of imported goods which are ordinarily used for more than one purpose so as to render them unfit for one or more of such purposes; and where any goods are so denatured or mutilated they shall be chargeable to duty at such rate as would be applicable if the goods had been imported in the denatured or mutilated form.

SECTION 25. Power to grant exemption from duty

(1) If the Central Government is satisfied that it is necessary in the public interest so to do, it may, by notification in the Official Gazette, exempt generally either absolutely or subject to such conditions (to be fulfilled before or after clearance) as may be specified in the notification goods of any specified description from the whole or any part of duty of customs leviable thereon.

(2) If the Central Government is satisfied that it is necessary in the public interest so to do, it may, by special order in each case, exempt from the payment of duty, under circumstances of an exceptional nature to be stated in such order, any goods on

which duty is leviable.

(2A) The Central Government may, if it considers it necessary or expedient so to do for the purpose of clarifying the scope or applicability of any notification issued under sub-section (1) or order issued under subsection (2), insert an explanation in such notification or order, as the case may be, by notification in the Official Gazette, at any time within one year of issue of the notification under sub-section (1) or order under sub-section (2), and every such explanation shall have effect as if it had always been the part of the first such notification or order, as the case may be.

(3) An exemption under sub-section (1) or sub-section (2) in respect of any goods from any part of the duty of customs leviable thereon (the duty of customs leviable thereon being hereinafter referred to as the statutory duty) may be granted by providing for the levy of a duty on such goods at a rate expressed in a form or method different from the form or method in which the statutory duty is leviable and any exemption granted in relation to any goods in the manner provided in this sub-section shall have effect subject to the condition that the duty of customs chargeable on such goods shall in no case exceed the statutory duty.

Explanation.– "Form or method" in relation to a rate of duty of customs, means the basis, namely, valuation, weight, number, length, area, volume or other measure with reference to which the duty is leviable.

(4) Every notification issued under sub-section (1) or sub-section (2A) shall,–
   (a) unless otherwise provided, come into force on the date of its issue by the Central Government for publication in the Official Gazette;
   (b) also be published and offered for sale on the date of its issue by the Directorate

of Publicity and Public Relations of the Board, New Delhi.

(5) Notwithstanding anything contained in sub-section (4), where a notification comes into force on a date later than the date of its issue, the same shall be published and offered for sale by the said Directorate of Publicity and Public Relations on a date on or before the date on which the said notification comes into force.

(6) Notwithstanding anything contained in this Act, no duty shall be collected if the amount of duty leviable is equal to, or less than, one hundred rupees.

SECTION 26. Refund of export duty in certain cases

Where on the exportation of any goods any duty has been paid, such duty shall be refunded to the person by whom or on whose behalf it was paid, if –
(a) the goods are returned to such person otherwise than by way of re-sale;
(b) the goods are re-imported within one year from the date of exportation; and
(c) an application for refund of such duty is made before the expiry of six months from the date on which the proper officer makes an order for the clearance of the goods.

SECTION 26A. Refund of import duty in certain cases

(1) Where on the importation of any goods capable of being easily identified as such imported goods, any duty has been paid on clearance of such goods for home consumption, such duty shall be refunded to the person by whom or on whose behalf it was paid, if –
   (a) the goods are found to be defective or otherwise not in conformity with the specifications agreed upon between the importer and the supplier of goods:

Provided that the goods have not been worked, repaired or used after importation except where such use was indispensable to discover the defects or non-conformity with the specifications;

(b) the goods are identified to the satisfaction of the Assistant Commissioner of Customs or Deputy Commissioner of Customs as the goods which were imported;

(c) the importer does not claim drawback under any other provisions of this Act; and

(d) (i) the goods are exported; or

(ii) the importer relinquishes his title to the goods and abandons them to customs; or

(iii) such goods are destroyed or rendered commercially valueless in the presence of the proper officer, in such manner as may be prescribed and within a period not exceeding thirty days from the date on which the proper officer makes an order for the clearance of imported goods for home consumption under section 47:

Provided that the period of thirty days may, on sufficient cause being shown, be extended by the Commissioner of Customs for a period not exceeding three months:

Provided further that nothing contained in this section shall apply to the goods regarding which an offence appears to have been committed under this Act or any other law for the time being in force.

(2) An application for refund of duty shall be made before the expiry of six months from the relevant date in such form and in such manner as may be prescribed.

Explanation.– For the purposes of this sub-section, "relevant date" means,–

a) in cases where the goods are exported out of India, the date on which the proper officer makes an order permitting clearance and loading of goods for exportation under section 51;

b) in cases where the title to the goods is relinquished, the date of such relinquishment;

c) in cases where the goods are destroyed or rendered commercially valueless, the date of such destruction or rendering of goods commercially valueless.

(3) No refund under sub-section (1) shall be allowed in respect of perishable goods and goods which have exceeded their shelf life or their recommended storage-before-use period.

(4) The Board may, by notification in the Official Gazette, specify any other condition subject to which the refund under sub-section (1) may be allowed.

SECTION 27. Claim for refund of duty

(1) Any person claiming refund of any duty or interest, –

(a) paid by him; or

(b) borne by him, may make an application in such form and manner as may be prescribed for such refund to the Assistant Commissioner of Customs or Deputy Commissioner of Customs, before the expiry of one year, from the date of payment of such duty or interest: Provided that where an application for refund has been made before the date on which the Finance Bill, 2011 receives the assent of the President, such application shall be deemed to have been made under subsection (1), as it stood before the date on which the Finance Bill, 2011 receives the assent of the President and the same shall be dealt with in accordance with the provisions of sub-section (2):

Provided further that the limitation of one year shall not apply where any duty or interest has been paid under protest. Explanation.— For the purposes of this sub-section, "the date of payment of duty or interest" in relation to a person, other than the importer, shall be construed as "the date of purchase of goods" by such person.

(1A) The application under sub-section (1) shall be accompanied by such documentary or other evidence (including the documents referred to in section 28C) as the applicant may furnish to establish that the amount of duty or interest, in relation to which such refund is claimed was collected from, or paid by, him and the incidence of such duty or interest, has not been passed on by him to any other person.

(1B) Save as otherwise provided in this section, the period of limitation of one year shall be computed in the following manner, namely:—
 (a) in the case of goods which are exempt from payment of duty by a special order issued under sub-section (2) of section 25, the limitation of one year shall be computed from the date of issue of such order;
 (b) where the duty becomes refundable as a consequence of any judgment, decree, order or direction of the appellate authority, Appellate Tribunal or any court, the limitation of one year shall be computed from the date of such judgment, decree, order or direction;
 (c) where any duty is paid provisionally under section 18, the limitation of one year shall be computed from the date of adjustment of duty after the final assessment thereof or in case of re-assessment, from the date of such re-assessment.

(2) If, on receipt of any such application, the Assistant Commissioner of Customs or Deputy Commissioner of Customs is satisfied that the whole or any part of the duty and interest, if any, paid on such duty paid by the applicant is refundable, he may make an order accordingly and the amount so determined shall be credited to

the Fund: Provided that the amount of duty and interest, if any, paid on such duty as determined by the Assistant Commissioner of Customs or Deputy Commissioner of Customs under the foregoing provisions of this subsection shall, instead of being credited to the Fund, be paid to the applicant, if such amount is relatable to—

(a) the duty and interest, if any, paid on such duty paid by the importer, or the exporter, as the case may be if he had not passed on the incidence of such duty and interest, if any, paid on such duty to any other person;

(b) the duty and interest, if any, paid on such duty on imports made by an individual for his personal use;

(c) the duty and interest, if any, paid on such duty borne by the buyer, if he had not passed on the incidence of such duty and interest, if any, paid on such duty to any other person;

(d) the export duty as specified in section 26;

(e) drawback of duty payable under sections 74 and 75;

(f) the duty and interest, if any, paid on such duty borne by any other such class of applicants as the Central Government may, by notification in the Official Gazette, specify:

Provided further that no notification under clause (f) of the first proviso shall be issued unless in the opinion of the Central Government the incidence of duty and interest, if any, paid on such duty has not been passed on by the persons concerned to any other person.

(3) Notwithstanding anything to the contrary contained in any judgment, decree, order or direction of the Appellate Tribunal, National Tax Tribunal or any Court or in any other provision of this Act or the regulations made thereunder or any other law for the time being in force, no refund shall be made except as provided in

sub-section (2).

(4) Every notification under clause (f) of the first proviso to sub-section (2) shall be laid before each House of Parliament, if it is sitting, as soon as may be after the issue of the notification, and, if it is not sitting, within seven days of its re-assembly, and the Central Government shall seek the approval of Parliament to the notification by a resolution moved within a period of fifteen days beginning with the day on which the notification is so laid before the House of the People and if Parliament makes any modification in the notification or directs that the notification should cease to have effect, the notification shall thereafter have effect only in such modified form or be of no effect, as the case may be, but without prejudice to the validity of anything previously done thereunder.

(5) For the removal of doubts, it is hereby declared that any notification issued under clause (f) of the first proviso to sub-section (2), including any such notification approved or modified under sub-section (4), may be rescinded by the Central Government at any time by notification in the Official Gazette.

SECTION 27A. Interest on delayed refunds

If any duty ordered to be refunded under sub-section (2) of section 27 to an applicant is not refunded within three months from the date of receipt of application under sub-section (1) of that section, there shall be paid to that applicant interest at such rate, not below five percent and not exceeding thirty percent per annum as is for the time being fixed by the Central Government by Notification in the Official Gazette, on such duty from the date immediately after the expiry of three months from the date of receipt of such application till the date of refund of such duty:

Provided that where any duty, ordered to be refunded under sub-section (2) of section 27 in respect of an application under sub-section (1) of that section made before the date on which the Finance Bill, 1995 receives the assent of the President, is not refunded within three months from such date, there shall be paid to the applicant interest under this section from the date immediately after three months from such date, till the date of refund of such duty.

Explanation.– Where any order of refund is made by the Commissioner (Appeals), Appellate Tribunal, National Tax Tribunal or any court against an order of the Assistant Commissioner of Customs or Deputy Commissioner of Customs under sub-section (2) of section 27, the order passed by the Commissioner (Appeals), Appellate Tribunal, National Tax Tribunal or as the case may be, by the court shall be deemed to be an order passed under that sub-section for the purposes of this section.

SECTION 28. Recovery of duties not levied or short-levied or erroneously refunded

(1) Where any duty has not been levied or has been short-levied or erroneously refunded, or any interest payable has not been paid, part-paid or erroneously refunded, for any reason other than the reasons of collusion or any wilful mis-statement or suppression of facts, –
   (a) the proper officer shall, within one year from the relevant date, serve notice on the person chargeable with the duty or interest which has not been so levied or which has been short-levied or short-paid or to whom the refund has erroneously been made, requiring him to show cause why he should not pay the amount specified in the notice;
   (b) the person chargeable with the duty or interest, may pay before service of notice under clause (a) on the basis of, – (i) his own ascertainment of such

duty; or (ii) the duty ascertained by the proper officer, the amount of duty along with the interest payable thereon under section 28AA or the amount of interest which has not been so paid or part-paid.

(2) The person who has paid the duty along with interest or amount of interest under clause (b) of sub-section (1) shall inform the proper officer of such payment in writing, who, on receipt of such information shall not serve any notice under clause (a) of that sub-section in respect of the duty or interest so paid or any penalty leviable under the provisions of this Act or the rules made thereunder in respect of such duty or interest.

(3) Where the proper officer is of the opinion that the amount paid under clause (b) of sub-section (1) falls short of the amount actually payable, then, he shall proceed to issue the notice as provided for in clause (a) of that sub-section in respect of such amount which falls short of the amount actually payable in the manner specified under that sub-section and the period of one year shall be computed from the date of receipt of information under sub-section (2).

(4) Where any duty has not been levied or has been short-levied or erroneously refunded, or interest payable has not been paid, part-paid or erroneously refunded, by reason of, — (a) collusion; or (b) any wilful mis-statement; or (c) suppression of facts, by the importer or the exporter or the agent or employee of the importer or exporter, the proper officer shall, within five years from the relevant date, serve notice on the person chargeable with duty or interest which has not been so levied or which has been so short-levied or short-paid or to whom the refund has erroneously been made, requiring him to show cause why he should not pay the amount specified in the notice.

(5) Where any duty has not been levied or has been short-levied or the interest has not been charged or has been part-paid or the duty or interest has been erroneously refunded by reason of collusion or any wilful mis-statement or suppression of facts by the importer or the exporter or the agent or the employee of the importer or the exporter, to whom a notice has been served under sub-section (4) by the proper officer, such person may pay the duty in full or in part, as may be accepted by him, and the interest payable thereon under section 28AA and the penalty equal to twenty-five percent. of the duty specified in the notice or the duty so accepted by that person, within thirty days of the receipt of the notice and inform the proper officer of such payment in writing.

(6) Where the importer or the exporter or the agent or the employee of the importer or the exporter, as the case may be, has paid duty with interest and penalty under sub-section (5), the proper officer shall determine the amount of duty or interest and on determination, if the proper officer is of the opinion – (i) that the duty with interest and penalty has been paid in full, then, the proceedings in respect of such person or other persons to whom the notice is served under sub-section (1) or sub-section (4), shall, without prejudice to the provisions of sections 135, 135A and 140 be deemed to be conclusive as to the matters stated therein; or (ii) that the duty with interest and penalty that has been paid falls short of the amount actually payable, then the proper officer shall proceed to issue the notice as provided for in clause (a) of sub-section (1) in respect of such amount which falls short of the amount actually payable in the manner specified under that sub-section and the period of one year shall be computed from the date of receipt of information under sub-section (5).

(7) In computing the period of one year referred to in clause (a) of sub-section (1) or five years referred to in sub-section (4), the period during which there was any

stay by an order of a court or tribunal in respect of payment of such duty or interest shall be excluded.

(8) The proper officer shall, after allowing the concerned person an opportunity of being heard and after considering the representation, if any, made by such person, determine the amount of duty or interest due from such person not being in excess of the amount specified in the notice.

(9) The proper officer shall determine the amount of duty or interest under sub-section (8), − (a) within six months from the date of notice in respect of cases falling under clause (a) of subsection (1); (b) within one year from the date of notice in respect of cases falling under sub-section (4).

(10) Where an order determining the duty is passed by the proper officer under this section, the person liable to pay the said duty shall pay the amount so determined along with the interest due on such amount whether or not the amount of interest is specified separately.

Explanation.− For the purposes of this section, "relevant date" means,− (a) in a case where duty is not levied, or interest is not charged, the date on which the proper officer makes an order for the clearance of goods; (b) in a case where duty is provisionally assessed under section 18, the date of adjustment of duty after the final assessment thereof; (c) in a case where duty or interest has been erroneously refunded, the date of refund; (d) in any other case, the date of payment of duty or interest.

SECTION 28A. Power not to recover duties not levied or short-levied as a result of general practice

(1) Notwithstanding anything contained in this Act, if the Central Government is satisfied:

    (a) that a practice was, or is, generally prevalent regarding levy of duty (including non-levy thereof) on any goods imported into, or exported from, India; and

    (b) that such goods were, or are, liable — (i) to duty, in cases where according to the said practice the duty was not, or is not being, levied, or (ii) to a higher amount of duty than what was, or is being, levied, according to the said practice, then, the Central Government may, by notification in the Official Gazette, direct that the whole of the duty payable on such goods, or, as the case may be, the duty in excess of that payable on such goods, but for the said practice, shall not be required to be paid in respect of the goods on which the duty was not, or is not being, levied, or was, or is being, short-levied, in accordance with the said practice.

(2) Where any notification under sub-section (1) in respect of any goods has been issued, the whole of the duty paid on such goods, or, as the case may be, the duty paid in excess of that payable on such goods, which would not have been paid if the said notification had been in force, shall be dealt with in accordance with the provisions of sub-section (2) of section 27:

Provided that the person claiming the refund of such duty or, as the case may be, excess duty, makes an application in this behalf to the Assistant Commissioner of Customs or Deputy Commissioner of Customs, in the form referred to in sub-section (1) of section 27, before the expiry of six months from the date of issue of the said notification.

SECTION 28AA Interest on delayed payment of duty

(1) Notwithstanding anything contained in any judgment, decree, order or direction of any court, Appellate Tribunal or any authority or in any other provision of this Act or the rules made there under, the person, who is liable to pay duty in accordance with the provisions of section 28, shall, in addition to such duty, be liable to pay interest, if any, at the rate fixed under sub-section (2), whether such payment is made voluntarily or after determination of the duty under that section.

(2) Interest at such rate not below ten percent. and not exceeding thirty-six percent. per annum, as the Central Government may, by notification in the Official Gazette, fix, shall be paid by the person liable to pay duty in terms of section 28 and such interest shall be calculated from the first day of the month succeeding the month in which the duty ought to have been paid or from the date of such erroneous refund, as the case may be, up to the date of payment of such duty.

(3) Notwithstanding anything contained in sub-section (1), no interest shall be payable where,– (a) the duty becomes payable consequent to the issue of an order, instruction or direction by the Board under section 151A; and (b) such amount of duty is voluntarily paid in full, within forty-five days from the date of issue of such order, instruction or direction, without reserving any right to appeal against the said payment at any subsequent stage of such payment.

SECTION 28B. Duties collected from the buyer to be deposited with the Central Government

(1) Notwithstanding anything to the contrary contained in any order or direction of the Appellate Tribunal, National Tax Tribunal or any Court or in any other provision of

this Act or the regulations made thereunder, every person who is liable to pay duty under this Act and has collected any amount in excess of the duty assessed or determined or paid on any goods under this Act from the buyer of such goods in any manner as representing duty of customs, shall forthwith pay the amount so collected to the credit of the Central Government.

(1A) Every person who has collected any amount in excess of the duty assessed or determined or paid on any goods or has collected any amount as representing duty of customs on any goods which are wholly exempt or are chargeable to nil rate of duty from any person in any manner, shall forthwith pay the amount so collected to the credit of the Central Government.

(2) Where any amount is required to be paid to the credit of the Central Government under sub-section (1) or sub-section (1A), as the case may be, and which has not been so paid, the proper officer may serve on the person liable to pay such amount, a notice requiring him to show cause why he should not pay the amount, as specified in the notice to the credit of the Central Government.

(3) The proper officer shall, after considering the representation, if any, made by the person on whom the notice is served under sub-section (2), determine the amount due from such person (not being in excess of the amount specified in the notice) and thereupon such person shall pay the amount so determined.

(4) The amount paid to the credit of the Central Government under sub-section (1) or sub-section (1A) or sub-section (3) as the case may be, shall be adjusted against the duty payable by the person on finalisation of assessment or any other proceeding for determination of the duty relating to the goods referred to in subsection (1) or sub-section (1A).

(5) Where any surplus is left after the adjustment made under sub-section (4), the amount of such surplus shall either be credited to the Fund or, as the case may be, refunded to the person who has borne the incidence of such amount, in accordance with the provisions of section 27 and such person may make an application under that section in such cases within six months from the date of the public notice to be issued by the Assistant Commissioner of Customs for the refund of such surplus amount.

SECTION 28BA. Provisional attachment to protect revenue in certain cases

(1) Where, during the pendency of any proceeding under section 28 or section 28B, the proper officer is of the opinion that for the purpose of protecting the interests of revenue, it is necessary so to do, he may, with the previous approval of the Commissioner of Customs, by order in writing, attach provisionally any property belonging to the person on whom notice is served under sub-section (1) of section 28 or sub-section (2) of section 28B, as the case may be, in accordance with the rules made in this behalf under section 142.

(2) Every such provisional attachment shall cease to have effect after the expiry of a period of six months from the date of the order made under sub-section (1):

Provided that the Chief Commissioner of Customs may, for reasons to be recorded in writing, extend the aforesaid period by such further period or periods as he thinks fit, so, however, that the total period of extension shall not in any case exceed two years:

Provided further that where an application for settlement of case under section 127B is made to the Settlement Commission, the period commencing from the date on which such application is made and ending with the date on which an order under sub-section (1) of section 127C is made shall be excluded from the period specified in the preceding proviso. THE CUSTOMS ACT, 1962 (52 of 1962)

CHAPTER VA INDICATING AMOUNT OF DUTY IN THE PRICE OF GOODS, ETC., FOR PURPOSE OF REFUND

SECTION 28C. Price of goods to indicate the amount of duty paid thereon

Notwithstanding anything contained in this Act or any other law for the time being in force, every person who is liable to pay duty on any goods shall, at the time of clearance of the goods, prominently indicate in all the documents relating to assessment, sales invoice, and other like documents, the amount of such duty which will form part of the price at which such goods are to be sold.

SECTION 28D. Presumption that incidence of duty has been passed on to the buyer

Every person who has paid the duty on any goods under this Act shall, unless the contrary is proved by him, be deemed to have passed on the full incidence of such duty to the buyer of such goods.

CHAPTER VB ADVANCE RULINGS SECTION

28E. Definitions

In this Chapter, unless the context otherwise requires, —
(a) "activity" means import or export;
(b) "advance ruling" means the determination, by the Authority, of a question of law or fact specified in the application regarding the liability to pay duty in relation to an activity which is proposed to be undertaken, by the applicant;
(c) "applicant" means — (i) (a) a non-resident setting up a joint venture in India in collaboration with a non-resident or resident; or (b) a resident setting up a joint venture in India in collaboration with a non-resident; or (c) a wholly owned subsidiary Indian company, of which the holding company is a foreign company, who or which, as the case may be, proposes to undertake any business activity in India; (ii) a joint venture in India; or (iii) a resident falling within any such class or category of persons, as the Central Government may, by notification in the Official Gazette, specify in this behalf, and which or who, as the case may be, makes application for advance ruling under sub-section (1) of section 28H; Explanation. — For the purposes of this clause, "Joint venture in India" means a contractual arrangement whereby two or more persons undertake an economic activity which is subject to joint control and one or more of the participants or partners or equity holder is a non-resident having substantial interest in such arrangement.
(d) "application" means an application made to the Authority under sub-section (1) of section 28H;
(e) "authority" means the Authority for Advance Rulings (Central Excise, Customs & Service Tax) constituted under section 28F;
(f) "chairperson" means the Chairperson of the Authority;
(g) "member" means a Member of the Authority and includes the Chairperson; and

(h) "non-resident" "Indian company" and "foreign company" have the meanings respectively assigned to them in clauses (30), (26) and (23A) of section 2 of the Income-tax Act, 1961 (43 of 1961).

SECTION 28F. Authority for advance rulings

(1) The Central Government shall, by notification in the Official Gazette, constitute an Authority for giving advance rulings, to be called as "The Authority for Advance Rulings (Central Excise, Customs & Service Tax)"

(2) The Authority shall consist of the following Members appointed by the Central Government, namely: – (a) a Chairperson, who is a retired Judge of the Supreme Court; (b) an officer of the Indian Customs and Central Excise Service who is qualified to be a Member of the Board; (c) an officer of the Indian Legal Service who is, or is qualified to be, an Additional Secretary to the Government of India.

(2A) Notwithstanding anything contained in sub-sections (1) and (2), or any other law for the time being in force, the Central Government may, by notification in the Official Gazette, authorize an Authority constituted under section 245-O of the Income-tax Act, 1961 (43 of 1961), to act as an Authority under this Chapter.

(2B) On and from the date of publication of notification under sub-section (2A), the Authority constituted under subsection (1) shall not exercise jurisdiction under this Chapter.

(2C) For the purposes of sub-section (2A), the reference to "an officer of the Indian Revenue Service who is qualified to be a Member of Central Board of Direct Taxes" in clause (b) of sub-section (2) of section 245-O of the Income-tax Act,

1961(43 of 1961) shall be construed as reference to "an officer of the Indian Customs and Central Excise Service who is qualified to be a Member of the Board" (2D) On and from the date of the authorisation of Authority under sub-section (2A), every application and proceeding pending before the Authority constituted under sub-section (1) shall stand transferred to the Authority so authorised from the stage at which such proceedings stood before the date of such authorisation.

(3) The salaries and allowances payable to, and the terms and conditions of service of, the Members shall be such as the Central Government may by rules determine.

(4) The Central Government shall provide the Authority with such officers and staff as may be necessary for the efficient exercise of the powers of the Authority under this Act.

(5) The office of the Authority shall be located in Delhi.

SECTION 28G. Vacancies, etc., not to invalidate proceedings

No proceeding before, or pronouncement of advance ruling by, the Authority under this Chapter shall be questioned or shall be invalid on the ground merely of the existence of any vacancy or defect in the constitution of the Authority.

SECTION 28H. Application for advance ruling

(1) An applicant desirous of obtaining an advance ruling under this Chapter may make an application in such form and in such manner as may be prescribed, stating the question on which the advance ruling is sought.

(2) The question on which the advance ruling is sought shall be in respect of, —
   (a) classification of goods under the Customs Tariff Act, 1975 (51 of 1975);
   (b) applicability of a notification issued under sub-section (1) of section 25, having a bearing on the rate of duty;
   (c) the principles to be adopted for the purposes of determination of value of the goods under the provisions of this Act.
   (d) applicability of notifications issued in respect of duties under this Act, the Customs Tariff Act, 1975 (51 of 1975) and any duty chargeable under any other law for the time being in force in the same manner as duty of customs leviable under this Act.
   (e) determination of origin of the goods in terms of the rules notified under the Customs Tariff Act, 1975 (51 of 1975) and matters relating thereto.

(3) The application shall be made in quadruplicate and be accompanied by a fee of two thousand five hundred rupees.

(4) An applicant may withdraw his application within thirty days from the date of the application.

SECTION 28I. Procedure on receipt of application.

(1) On receipt of an application, the Authority shall cause a copy thereof to be forwarded to the Commissioner of Customs and, if necessary, call upon him to furnish the relevant records:

Provided that where any records have been called for by the Authority in any case, such records shall, as soon as possible, be returned to the Commissioner of Customs.

(2) The Authority may, after examining the application and the records called for, by order, either allow or reject the application: Provided that the Authority shall not allow the application where the question raised in the application is
   (a) already pending in the applicant' case before any officer of customs, the Appellate Tribunal or any Court;
   (b) the same as in a matter already decided by the Appellate Tribunal or any Court : Provided further that no application shall be rejected under this sub-section unless an opportunity has been given to the applicant of being heard: Provided also that where the application is rejected, reasons for such rejection shall be given in the order.

(3) A copy of every order made under sub-section (2) shall be sent to the applicant and to the Commissioner of Customs.

(4) Where an application is allowed under sub-section (2), the Authority shall, after examining such further material as may be placed before it by the applicant or obtained by the Authority, pronounce its advance ruling on the question specified in the application.

(5) On a request received from the applicant, the Authority shall, before pronouncing its advance ruling, provide an opportunity to the applicant of being heard, either in person or through a duly authorised representative.

Explanation.− For the purposes of this sub-section, "authorised representative" shall have the meaning assigned to it in sub-section (2) of section 146A.

(6) The Authority shall pronounce its advance ruling in writing within ninety days of the receipt of application.

(7) A copy of the advance ruling pronounced by the Authority, duly signed by the Members and certified in the prescribed manner shall be sent to the applicant and to the Commissioner of Customs, as soon as may be, after such pronouncement.

SECTION 28J. Applicability of advance ruling

(1) The advance ruling pronounced by the Authority under section 28-I shall be binding only –
   (a) on the applicant who had sought it;
   (b) in respect of any matter referred to in sub-section (2) of section 28H;
   (c) on the Commissioner of Customs, and the customs authorities subordinate to him, in respect of the applicant.

(2) The advance ruling referred to in sub-section (1) shall be binding as aforesaid unless there is a change in law or facts on the basis of which the advance ruling has been pronounced.

SECTION 28K. Advance ruling to be void in certain circumstances

(1) Where the Authority finds, on a representation made to it by the Commissioner of Customs or otherwise, that an advance ruling pronounced by it under sub-section (6) of section 28-I has been obtained by the applicant by fraud or misrepresentation of facts, it may, by order, declare such ruling to be void ab initio and thereupon all the provisions of this Act shall apply (after excluding the period beginning with the date of such advance ruling and ending with the date of order under this sub-section) to the applicant as if such advance ruling had never been made.

(2) A copy of the order made under sub-section (1) shall be sent to the applicant and the Commissioner of Customs.

SECTION 28L. Powers of Authority

(1) The Authority shall, for the purpose of exercising its powers regarding discovery and inspection, enforcing the attendance of any person and examining him on oath, issuing commissions and compelling production of books of account and other records, have all the powers of a civil court under the Code of Civil Procedure, 1908 (5 of 1908).

(2) The Authority shall be deemed to be a civil court for the purposes of section 195, but not for the purposes of Chapter XXVI of the Code of Criminal Procedure, 1973 (2 of 1974), and every proceeding before the Authority shall be deemed to be a judicial proceeding within the meaning of sections 193 and 228, and for the purpose of section 196, of the Indian Penal Code (45 of 1860).

SECTION 28M. Procedure of Authority

The Authority shall, subject to the provisions of this Chapter, have power to regulate its own procedure in all matters arising out of the exercise of its powers under this Act.

CHAPTER VI PROVISIONS RELATING TO CONVEYANCES CARRYING IMPORTED OR EXPORTED GOODS

SECTION 29. Arrival of vessels and aircrafts in India

(1) The person-in-charge of a vessel or an aircraft entering India from any place outside India shall not cause or permit the vessel or aircraft to call or land—
   (a) for the first time after arrival in India; or
   (b) at any time while it is carrying passengers or cargo brought in that vessel or aircraft; at any place other than a customs port or a customs airport, as the case may be.

(2) The provisions of sub-section (1) shall not apply in relation to any vessel or aircraft which is compelled by accident, stress of weather or other unavoidable cause to call or land at a place other than a customs port or customs airport but the person-in-charge of any such vessel or aircraft—
   (a) shall immediately report the arrival of the vessel or the landing of the aircraft to the nearest customs officer or the officer-in-charge of a police station and shall on demand produce to him the log book belonging to the vessel or the aircraft;
   (b) shall not without the consent of any such officer permit any goods carried in the vessel or the aircraft to be unloaded from, or any of the crew or passengers to depart from the vicinity of, the vessel or the aircraft; and
   (c) shall comply with any directions given by any such officer with respect to any such goods, and no passenger or member of the crew shall, without the consent of any such officer, leave the immediate vicinity of the vessel or the aircraft:

Provided that nothing in this section shall prohibit the departure of any crew or passengers from the vicinity of, or the removal of goods from, the vessel or aircraft where the departure or removal is necessary for reasons of health, safety or the preservation of life or property.

SECTION 30. Delivery of import manifest or import report

(1) The person-in-charge of —
   (i) a vessel; or
   (ii) an aircraft; or
   (iii) a vehicle, carrying imported goods or any other person as may be specified by the Central Government, by notification in the Official Gazette, in this behalf shall, in the case of a vessel or an aircraft, deliver to the proper officer an import manifest prior to the arrival of the vessel or the aircraft, as the case may be, and in the case of a vehicle, an import report within twelve hours after its arrival in the customs station, in the prescribed form and if the import manifest or the import report or any part thereof, is not delivered to the proper officer within the time specified in this sub-section and if the proper officer is satisfied that there was no sufficient cause for such delay, the person-in-charge or any other person referred to in this sub-section, who caused such delay, shall be liable to a penalty not exceeding fifty thousand rupees.

Provided that, —
(a) in the case of a vessel or an aircraft, any such manifest may be delivered to the proper officer before the arrival of the vessel or aircraft;
(b) if the proper officer is satisfied that there was sufficient cause for not delivering the import manifest or import report or any part thereof within the time specified in this sub-section, he may accept it at any time thereafter.

(2) The person delivering the import manifest or import report shall at the foot thereof

make and subscribe to a declaration as to the truth of its contents.

(3) If the proper officer is satisfied that the import manifest or import report is in any way incorrect or incomplete, and that there was no fraudulent intention, he may permit it to be amended or supplemented.

SECTION 31. Imported goods not to be unloaded from vessel until entry inwards granted

(1) The master of a vessel shall not permit the unloading of any imported goods until an order has been given by the proper officer granting entry inwards to such vessel.

(2) No order under sub-section (1) shall be given until an import manifest has been delivered or the proper officer is satisfied that there was sufficient cause for not delivering it.

(3) Nothing in this section shall apply to the unloading of baggage accompanying a passenger or a member of the crew, mail bags, animals, perishable goods and hazardous goods.

SECTION 32. Imported goods not to be unloaded unless mentioned in import manifest or import report

No imported goods required to be mentioned under the regulations in an import manifest or import report shall, except with the permission of the proper officer, be unloaded at any customs station unless they are specified in such manifest or report for being unloaded at that customs station.

SECTION 33. Unloading and loading of goods at approved places only

Except with the permission of the proper officer, no imported goods shall be unloaded, and no export goods shall be loaded, at any place other than a place approved under clause (a) of section 8 for the unloading or loading of such goods.

SECTION 34. Goods not to be unloaded or loaded except under supervision of customs officer

Imported goodsshall not be unloaded from, and export goods shall not be loaded on, any conveyance except under the supervision of the proper officer:

Provided that the Board may, by notification in the Official Gazette, give general permission and the proper officer may in any particular case give special permission, for any goods or class of goods to be unloaded or loaded without the supervision of the proper officer.

SECTION 35. Restrictions on goods being water-borne

No imported goods shall be water-borne for being landed from any vessel, and no export goods which are not accompanied by a shipping bill, shall be water-borne for being shipped, unless the goods are accompanied by a boat-note in the prescribed form:

Provided that the Board may, by notification in the Official Gazette, give general permission, and the proper officer may in any particular case give special permission, for any goods or any class of goods to be water-borne without being accompanied by a boat-note.

SECTION 36. Restrictions on unloading and loading of goods on holidays, etc.

No imported goods shall be unloaded from, and no export goods shall be loaded on, any conveyance on any Sunday or on any holiday observed by the Customs Department or on any other day after the working hours, except after giving the prescribed notice and on payment of the prescribed fees, if any:

Provided that no fees shall be levied for the unloading and loading of baggage accompanying a passenger or a member of the crew, and mail bags.

SECTION 37. Power to board conveyances

The proper officer may, at any time, board any conveyance carrying imported goods or export goods and may remain on such conveyance for such period as he considers necessary.

SECTION 38. Power to require production of documents and ask questions

For the purposes of carrying out the provisions of this Act, the proper officer may require the person-in-charge of any conveyance or animal carrying imported goods or export goods to produce any document and to answer any questions and thereupon such person shall produce such documents and answer such questions.

SECTION 39. Export goods not to be loaded on vessel until entry-outwards granted

The master of a vessel shall not permit the loading of any export goods, other than baggage and mail bags, until an order has been given by the proper officer granting entry-outwards to such vessel.

SECTION 40. Export goods not to be loaded unless duly passed by proper officer

The person-in-charge of a conveyance shall not permit the loading at a customs station —
(a) of export goods, other than baggage and mail bags, unless a shipping bill or bill of export or a bill of transhipment, as the case may be, duly passed by the proper officer, has been handed over to him by the exporter;
(b) of baggage and mail bags, unless their export has been duly permitted by the proper officer.

SECTION 41. Delivery of export manifest or export report

(1) The person-in-charge of a conveyance carrying export goods shall, before departure of the conveyance from a customs station, deliver to the proper officer in the case of a vessel or aircraft, an export manifest, and in the case of a vehicle, an export report, in the prescribed form:
(2) The person delivering the export manifest or export report shall at the foot thereof make and subscribe to a declaration as to the truth of its contents.
(3) If the proper officer is satisfied that the export manifest or export report is in any way incorrect or incomplete and that there was no fraudulent intention, he may permit such manifest or report to be amended or supplemented.

SECTION 42. No conveyance to leave without written order

(1) The person-in-charge of a conveyance which has brought any imported goods or has loaded any export goods at a customs station shall not cause or permit the conveyance to depart from that customs station until a written order to that effect has been given by the proper officer.

(2) No such order shall be given until –
  (a) the person-in-charge of the conveyance has answered the questions put to him under section 38;
  (b) the provisions of section 41 have been complied with;
  (c) the shipping bills or bills of export, the bills of transhipment, if any, and such other documents as the proper officer may require have been delivered to him;
  (d) all duties leviable on any stores consumed in such conveyance, and all charges and penalties due in respect of such conveyance or from the person-in-charge thereof have been paid or the payment secured by such guarantee or deposit of such amount as the proper officer may direct;
  (e) the person-in-charge of the conveyance has satisfied the proper officer that no penalty is leviable on him under section 116 or the payment of any penalty that may be levied upon him under that section has been secured by such guarantee or deposit of such amount as the proper officer may direct;
  (f) in any case where any export goods have been loaded without payment of export duty or in contravention of any provision of this Act or any other law for the time being in force relating to export of goods, –
    (i) such goods have been unloaded, or
    (ii) where the Assistant Commissioner of Customs or Deputy Commissioner of Customs is satisfied that it is not practicable to unload such goods, the person-in-charge of the conveyance has given an undertaking, secured by

such guarantee or deposit of such amount as the proper officer may direct, for bringing back the goods to India.

SECTION 43. Exemption of certain classes of conveyances from certain provisions of this Chapter

(1) The provisions of sections 30, 41 and 42 shall not apply to a vehicle which carries no goods other than the luggage of its occupants.

(2) The Central Government may, by notification in the Official Gazette, exempt the following classes of conveyances from all or any of the provisions of this Chapter
   (a) conveyances belonging to the Government or any foreign Government;
   (b) vessels and aircraft which temporarily enter India by reason of any emergency

CHAPTER VII CLEARANCE OF IMPORTED GOODS AND EXPORT GOODS

SECTION 44. Chapter not to apply to baggage and postal articles

The provisions of this Chapter shall not apply to (a) baggage, and (b) goods imported or to be exported by post.

[Clearance of imported goods]

SECTION 45. Restrictions on custody and removal of imported goods

(1) Save as otherwise provided in any law for the time being in force, all imported goods unloaded in a customs area shall remain in the custody of such person as may be approved by the Commissioner of Customs until they are cleared for home consumption or are warehoused or are transhipped in accordance with the provisions of Chapter VIII.

(2) The person having custody of any imported goods in a customs area, whether under the provisions of sub-section (1) or under any law for the time being in force, —
 (a) shall keep a record of such goods and send a copy thereof to the proper officer;
 (b) shall not permit such goods to be removed from the customs area or otherwise dealt with, except under and in accordance with the permission in writing of the proper officer.

(3) Notwithstanding anything contained in any law for the time being in force, if any imported goods are pilferred after unloading thereof in a customs area while in the custody of a person referred to in sub-section (1), that person shall be liable to pay duty on such goods at the rate prevailing on the date of delivery of an import manifest or, as the case may be, an import report to the proper officer under section 30 for the arrival of the conveyance in which the said goods were carried.

SECTION 46. Entry of goods on importation

(1) The importer of any goods, other than goods intended for transit or transhipment,

shall make entry thereof by presenting electronically to the proper officer a bill of entry for home consumption or warehousing in the prescribed form:

Provided that the Commissioner of Customs may, in cases where it is not feasible to make entry by presenting electronically , allow an entry to be presented in any other manner:

Provided further that if the importer makes and subscribes to a declaration before the proper officer, to the effect that he is unable for want of full information to furnish all the particulars of the goods required under this sub-section, the proper officer may, pending the production of such information, permit him, previous to the entry thereof (a) to examine the goods in the presence of an officer of customs, or (b) to deposit the goods in a public warehouse appointed under section 57 without warehousing the same.

(2) Save as otherwise permitted by the proper officer, a bill of entry shall include all the goods mentioned in the bill of lading or other receipt given by the carrier to the consignor.

(3) A bill of entry under sub-section (1) may be presented at any time after the delivery of the import manifest or import report as the case maybe:

Provided that the Commissioner of Customs may in any special circumstances permit a bill of entry to be presented before the delivery of such report:

Provided further that a bill of entry may be presented even before the delivery of such manifest if the vessel or the aircraft by which the goods have been shipped for importation into India is expected to arrive within thirty days from the date of such presentation.

(4) The importer while presenting a bill of entry shall at the foot thereof make and subscribe to a declaration as to the truth of the contents of such bill of entry and shall, in support of such declaration, produce to the proper officer the invoice, if any, relating to the imported goods.

(5) If the proper officer is satisfied that the interests of revenue are not prejudicially affected and that there was no fraudulent intention, he may permit substitution of a bill of entry for home consumption for a bill of entry for warehousing or vice versa.

SECTION 47. Clearance of goods for home consumption

(1) Where the proper officer is satisfied that any goods entered for home consumption are not prohibited goods and the importer has paid the import duty, if any, assessed thereon and any charges payable under this Act in respect of the same, the proper officer may make an order permitting clearance of the goods for home consumption.

(2) Where the importer fails to pay the import duty under sub-section (1) within five days excluding holidays from the date on which the bill of entry is returned to him for payment of duty, he shall pay interest at such rate, not below ten percent and not exceeding thirty six percent. perannum, as is for the time being fixed by the Central Government, by notification in the Official Gazette, on such duty till the date of payment of the said duty:

Provided that where the bill of entry is returned for payment of duty before the commencement of the Customs (Amendment) Act, 1991 and the importer has not paid such duty before such commencement, the date of return of such bill of entry to him shall be deemed to be the date of such commencement for the purpose of this section.

Provided further that if the Board is satisfied that it is necessary in the public interest so to do, it may, by order for reasons to be recorded, waive the whole or part of any interest payable under this section.

SECTION 48. Procedure in case of goods not cleared, warehoused, or transhipped within thirty days after unloading

If any goods brought into India from a place outside India are not cleared for home consumption or warehoused or transhipped within thirty days from the date of the unloading thereof at a customs station or within such further time as the proper officer may allow or if the title to any imported goods is relinquished, such goods may, after notice to the importer and with the permission of the proper officer be sold by the person having the custody thereof :

Provided that —
(a) animals, perishable goods and hazardous goods, may, with the permission of the proper officer, be sold at any time;
(b) arms and ammunition may be sold at such time and place and in such manner as the Central Government may direct.

Explanation.— In this section, "arms" and "ammunition" have the meanings respectively assigned to them in the Arms Act, 1959 (54 of 1959).

SECTION 49. Storage of imported goods in warehouse pending clearance

Where in the case of any imported goods, whether dutiable or not, entered for home consumption, the Assistant Commissioner of Customs or Deputy Commissioner of Customs is satisfied on the application of the importer that the goods cannot be cleared within a reasonable time, the goods may, pending clearance, be permitted to be stored in a public warehouse, or in a private warehouse if facilities for deposit in a public warehouse are not available; but such goods shall not be deemed to be warehoused goods for the purposes of this Act, and accordingly the provisions of Chapter IX shall not apply to such goods.

[Clearance of export goods]

SECTION 50. Entry of goods for exportation

(1) The exporter of any goods shall make entry thereof by presenting electronically to the proper officer in the case of goods to be exported in a vessel or aircraft, a shipping bill, and in the case of goods to be exported by land, a bill of export in the prescribed form.

Provided that the Commissioner of Customs may, in cases where it is not feasible to make entry by presenting electronically, allow an entry to be presented in any other manner.

(2) The exporter of any goods, while presenting a shipping bill or bill of export, shall make and subscribe to a declaration as to the truth of its contents.

SECTION 51. Clearance of goods for exportation

Where the proper officer is satisfied that any goods entered for export are not prohibited goods and the exporter has paid the duty, if any, assessed thereon and any charges payable under this Act in respect of the same, the proper officer may make an order permitting clearance and loading of the goods for exportation.

CHAPTER VIII GOODS IN TRANSIT

SECTION 52. Chapter not to apply to baggage, postal articles and stores

The provisions of this Chapter shall not apply to (a) baggage, (b) goods imported by post, and (c) stores.

SECTION 53. Transit of certain goods without payment of duty

Subject to the provisions of section 11, any goods imported in a conveyance and mentioned in the import manifest or the import report, as the case may be, as for transit in the same conveyance to any place outside India or any customs station may be allowed to be so transited without payment of duty.

SECTION 54. Transhipment of certain goods without payment of duty

(1) Where any goods imported into a customs station are intended for transhipment, a bill of transhipment shall be presented to the proper officer in the prescribed form.

Provided that where the goods are being transhipped under an international treaty or bilateral agreement between the Government of India and Government of a foreign country, a declaration for transhipment instead of a bill of transhipment shall be presented to the proper officer in the prescribed form.

(2) Subject to the provisions of section 11, where any goods imported into a customs station are mentioned in the import manifest or the import report, as the case may be, as for transhipment to any place outside India, such goods may be allowed to be so transhipped without payment of duty.

(3) Where any goods imported into a customs station are mentioned in the import manifest or the import report, as the case may be, as for transhipment (a) to any major port as defined in the Indian Ports Act, 1908 (15 of 1908), or the customs airport at Mumbai, Calcutta, Delhi or Chennai or any other customs port or customs airport which the Board may, by notification in the Official Gazette, specify in this behalf, or (b) to any other customs station and the proper officer is satisfied that the goods are bona fide intended for transhipment to such customs station, the proper officer may allow the goods to be transhipped, without payment of duty, subject to such conditions as may be prescribed for the due arrival of such goods at the customs station to which transhipment is allowed.

SECTION 55. Liability of duty on goods transited under section 53 or transhipped under section 54

Where any goods are allowed to be transited under section 53 or transhipped under sub-section (3) of section 54 to any customs station, they shall, on their arrival at such station, be liable to duty and shall be entered in like manner as goods are entered on the first importation thereof and the provisions of this Act and any rules and regulations shall, so far as may be, apply in relation to such goods.

SECTION 56. Transport of certain classes of goods subject to prescribed conditions

Imported goods may be transported without payment of duty from one land customs station to another, and any goods may be transported from one part of India to another part through any foreign territory, subject to such conditions as may be prescribed for the due arrival of such goods at the place of destination.

CHAPTER X DRAWBACK

SECTION 74. Drawback allowable on re-export of duty-paid goods

(1) When any goods capable of being easily identified which have been imported into India and upon which any duty has been paid on importation, −
  (i) are entered for export and the proper officer makes an order permitting clearance and loading of the goods for exportation under section 51; or
  (ii) are to be exported as baggage and the owner of such baggage, for the purpose of clearing it, makes a declaration of its contents to the proper officer under section 77 (which declaration shall be deemed to be an entry for export for the purposes of this section) and such officer makes an order permitting clearance of the goods for exportation; or
  (iii) are entered for export by post under section 82 and the proper officer makes an order permitting clearance of the goods for exportation, ninety-eight percent of such duty shall, except as otherwise hereinafter provided, be re-paid as drawback, if − (a) the goods are identified to the satisfaction of the Assistant Commissioner of Customs or Deputy Commissioner of Customs as the goods which were imported; and (b) the goods are entered for export within two years from the date of payment of duty on the importation thereof:

Provided that in any particular case the aforesaid period of two years may, on sufficient cause being shown, be extended by the Board by such further period as it may deem fit.

(2) Notwithstanding anything contained in sub-section (1), the rate of drawback in the case of goods which have been used after the importation thereof shall be such as the Central Government, having regard to the duration of use, depreciation in value and other relevant circumstances, may, by notification in the Official Gazette, fix.

(3) The Central Government may make rules for the purpose of carrying out the provisions of this section and, in particular, such rules may –
   (a) provide for the manner in which the identity of goods imported in different consignments which are ordinarily stored together in bulk, may be established;
   (b) specify the goods which shall be deemed to be not capable of being easily identified; and
   (c) provide for the manner and the time within which a claim for payment of drawback is to be filed.

(4) For the purposes of this section –
   (a) goods shall be deemed to have been entered for export on the date with reference to which the rate of duty is calculated under section 16;
   (b) in the case of goods assessed to duty provisionally under section 18, the date of payment of the provisional duty shall be deemed to be the date of payment of duty.

SECTION 75. Drawback on imported materials used in the manufacture of goods which are exported

(1) Where it appears to the Central Government that in respect of goods of any class or description manufactured, processed or on which any operation has been carried out in India, being goods which have been entered for export and in respect of which an order permitting the clearance and loading thereof for exportation has been made under section 51 by the proper officer, or being goods entered for export by post under section 82 and in respect of which an order permitting clearance for exportation has been made by the proper officer, a drawback should be allowed of duties of customs chargeable under this Act on any imported materials of a class or description used in the manufacture or processing of such goods or carrying out any operation on such goods, the Central Government may, by notification in the Official Gazette, direct that drawback shall be allowed in respect of such goods in accordance with, and subject to, the rules made under sub-section (2).

Provided that no drawback shall be allowed under this sub-section in respect of any of the aforesaid goods which the Central Government may, by rules made under sub-section (2), specify, if the export value of such goods or class of goods is less than the value of the imported materials used in the manufacture or processing of such goods or carrying out any operation on such goods or class of goods, or is not more than such percentage of the value of the imported materials used in the manufacture or processing of such goods or carrying out any operation on such goods or class of goods as the Central Government may, by notification in the Official Gazette, specify in this behalf:

Provided further that where any drawback has been allowed on any goods under this sub-section and the sale proceeds in respect of such goods are not received by or on behalf of the exporter in India within the time allowed under the Foreign Exchange Management Act, 1999 (42 of 1999), such drawback shall except under such circumstances or such conditions as the Central Government may, by rule, specify be deemed never to have been allowed and the Central Government may, by rules made under sub-section (2), specify the procedure for the recovery or adjustment of the amount of such drawback.

(1A) Where it appears to the Central Government that the quantity of a particular material imported into India is more than the total quantity of like material that has been used in the goods manufactured, processed or on which any operation has been carried out in India and exported outside India, then, the Central Government may, by notification in the Official Gazette, declare that so much of the material as is contained in the goods exported shall, for the purpose of sub-section (1), be deemed to be imported material.

(2) The Central Government may make rules for the purpose of carrying out the provisions of sub-section (1) and, in particular, such rules may provide –

   (a) for the payment of drawback equal to the amount of duty actually paid on the imported materials used in the manufacture or processing of the goods or carrying out any operation on the goods or as is specified in the rules as the average amount of duty paid on the materials of that class or description used in the manufacture or processing of export goods or carrying out any operation on export goods of that class or description either by manufacturers generally or by persons processing or carrying on any operation generally or by any particular manufacturer or particular person carrying on any process or other operation, and interest if any payable thereon;

   (aa) for specifying the goods in respect of which no drawback shall be allowed;

(ab) for specifying the procedure for recovery or adjustment of the amount of any drawback which had been allowed under sub-section (1) or interest chargeable thereon;

(b) for the production of such certificates, documents and other evidence in support of each claim of drawback as may be necessary;

(c) for requiring the manufacturer or the person carrying out any process or other operation to give access to every part of his manufactory to any officer of customs specially authorised in this behalf by the Assistant Commissioner of Customs or Deputy Commissioner of Customs to enable such authorised officer to inspect the processes of manufacture, process or any other operation carried out and to verify by actual check or otherwise the statements made in support of the claim for drawback.

(d) for the manner and the time within which the claim for payment of drawback may be filed;

(3) The power to make rules conferred by sub-section (2) shall include the power to give drawback with retrospective effect from a date not earlier than the date of changes in the rates of duty on inputs used in the export goods.

SECTION 75A. Interest on drawback

(1) Where any drawback payable to a claimant under section 74 or section 75 is not paid within a period of one month from the date of filing a claim for payment of such drawback, there shall be paid to that claimant in addition to the amount of drawback, interest at the rate fixed under section 27A from the date after the expiry of the said period of one month till the date of payment of such drawback:

(2) Where any drawback has been paid to the claimant erroneously or it becomes

otherwise recoverable under this Act or the rules made thereunder, the claimant shall, within a period of two months from the date of demand, pay in addition to the said amount of drawback, interest at the rate fixed under section 28AB and the amount of interest shall be calculated for the period beginning from the date of payment of such drawback to the claimant till the date of recovery of such drawback.

SECTION 76. Prohibition and regulation of drawback in certain cases

(1) Notwithstanding anything hereinbefore contained, no drawback shall be allowed
   (a) Omitted
   (b) in respect of any goods the market-price of which is less than the amount of drawback due thereon;
   (c) where the drawback due in respect of any goods is less than fifty rupees.

(2) Without prejudice to the provisions of sub-section (1), if the Central Government is of opinion that goods of any specified description in respect of which drawback may be claimed under this Chapter are likely to be smuggled back into India, it may, by notification in the Official Gazette, direct that drawback shall not be allowed in respect of such goods or may be allowed subject to such restrictions and conditions as may be specified in the notification.

부록 Ⅵ. 통관 관련서류 양식

1. GR form: Exchange Control Declaration form

EXCHANGE CONTROL DECLARATION (GR) FORM NO.

Original

	Exporter			Invoice No.& Date	SB No.& Date	
				AR4/AR4A No.& Date		
				Q/Cert No.& Date	Importer-Exporter Code No.	
	Consignee					
				Export Trade Control	If export under:	
					Deferred Credit [ ]	
					Joint Ventures [ ]	
					Rupee Credit [ ]	
					Others [ ]	
					RBI's Approval/Cir.No. & Date	
	Custom House Agent L/C.No.					
	Pre-Carriage by	Place of Receipt by Pre-Carrier			Type of shipment : Outright Sale [ ] Consignment Export [ ]	
	Vessel/Flight No.	Rotatio No.			Others [ ] (Specify)	
		Port of Loading		Nature of Contract:CIF[ ]/C&F [ ]/FOB [ ] Other (Specify) [ ]		
	Port of Discharge	Country of Destination		Exchange Rate U/S 14 of CA Currency of invoice		
S.No	Marks & No. No. & Kind of Pkgs.		Statistical Code & Description of Goods		Quantity	Value FOB
	Container Nos.					
	Net Weight					
	Gross Weight					
	Total FOB Value in words					
	Analysis of Export Value		Currency Amount	Full export value OR where not ascertainable, the value which exporter expects to receive on the sale of goods.		
	FOB Value					
	Freight					
	Insurance			Currency		
	Commission		Rate			
	Discount			Amount		
	Other Deductions					

2

EXCHANGE CONTROL DECLARATION (GR) FORM NO.

Is Export under L/C arrangements? Yes [ ] No [ ]	**FOR CUSTOMS**
If yes, name of advising bank in India	Customs Assessable value Rs.
	(Rupees .
	....

Bank through which payment is to be received	
	Export Value Verified
	Customs Appraiser
Whether Payment is to be received through the ACU YES/NO	Date of Shipment Customs Appraiser

Declaration under Foreign Exchange Management Act, 1999: I/We hereby declare that I/We am/are the *SELLER/CONSIGNOR of the goods in respect of which this declaration is made and that the particulars given above are true and that a)*the value as contracted with the buyer is the same as the full export value declared overleaf/ b) *the full export value of the goods is not ascertainable at the time of export and that the value declared is that which I/We, having regard to the prevailing market-conditions, expect to receive on the sale of goods in the overseas market.

I/We undertake that I/We will deliver to the bank named herein the foreign exchange representing the full export value of the goods on or before @ .... in the manner soecified in the Regulations under the Act. I/We further declare that I/We am/are resident in India and I/We have a place of business in India.

I/We* am/are OR am/are not in Caution List of the Reserve Bank of India.

....
Date................   (Signature of Exporter)

@ State appropriate date of delivery which must be within six months from the date of shipment, but for exports to warehouses established outside India with the permission of the Reserve Bank, the date of delivery must be within fifteen months.

* Strike out whichever is not applicable

SPACE FOR USE BY RESERVE BANK OF INDIA

EXCHANGE CONTROL DECLARATION (GR) FORM NO.

Duplicate

Exporter		Invoice No.& Date	SB No.& Date
		AR4/AR4A No.& Date	
		Q/Cert No.& Date	Importer-Exporter Code No.
Consignee			
		Export Trade Control	If export under:
			Deferred Credit [ ]
			Joint Ventures [ ]
			Rupee Credit [ ]
			Others [ ]
			RBI's Approval/Cir.No. & Date
Custom House Agent L/C.No.			
Pre-Carriage by	Place of Receipt By Pre-Carrier		Type of shipment : Outright Sale [ ]
			Consignment Export [ ]
Vessel/Flight No.	Rotation No.		Others [ ] (Specify)
	Port of Loading		Nature of Contract:CIF[ ]/C&F [ ]/FOB [ ] Other (Specify) [ ]
Port of Discharge	Country of Destination		Exchange Rate U/S 14 of CA Currency of invoice

S.No	Marks & No. No. & Kind of Pkgs.	Statistical Code & Description of Goods	Quantity	Value FOB
	Container Nos.			
	Net Weight			
	Gross Weight			
	Total FOB Value in words			

Analysis of Export Value		Currency Amount		Full export value OR where not ascertainable, the value which exporter expects to receive on the sale of goods.
FOB Value				
Freight				
Insurance				Currency	
Commission		Rate		
Discount				Amount	
Other Deductions				

2

EXCHANGE CONTROL DECLARATION (GR) FORM NO.

Is Export under L/C arrangements? Yes [ ] No [ ]	**FOR CUSTOMS**
If yes, name of advising bank in India	Customs Assessable value Rs.

		(Rupees .	
		....	
Bank through which payment is to be received			

* (Write the name of the concerned Indian Authorised Dealer Branch.) Any other manner of receipt (Specify)..							
					(Stamp & Signature of authorised dealer) Date:................................... Address:..			

overleaf/ b) *the full export value of the goods is not ascertainable at the time of export and that the value declared is that which I/We, having regard to the prevailing market-conditions, expect to receive on the sale of goods in the overseas market.

I/We undertake that I/We will deliver to the bank named herein the foreign exchange representing the full export value of the goods on or before @ .... in the manner specified in the Regulation made under the Act.

I/We further declare that I/We am/are resident in India and I/We have a place of business in India.

I/We* am/are OR am/are not in Caution List of the Reserve Bank of India.
....
Date................   (Signature of Exporter)

@ State appropriate date of delivery which must be within six months from the date of shipment, but for exports to warehouses established outside India with the permission of the Reserve Bank, the date of delivery must be within fifteen months.

* Strike out whichever is not applicable

FOR AUTHORISED DEALER'S USE
Uniform Code Number.........................
Indicate ( ) in the box applicable Date of (I) negotiation (ii) receipt for collection. Bill No..........................
Type of Bill* (i)DA[ ]/(ii)DP [ ]/(iii)Others [ ] ....(Specify)
Type of shipment:*(i) Firm Sale Contract [ ]/(ii)Consignment Basis [ ]/
(iii)Others [ ] ....(Specify)
The GR Form was included in the Statement sent to the Reserve Bank with
the R Return for the fortnight ending..........................sent on......................
We certify and confirm that we have received the total amount of............................
                                             (Currency) (amount)
as under being the proceeds of exports declared on this form.

3

Date of receipt	Currency	Credit to Nostro Account in------------ ------Country		Debit to NR Rupee Account of a Bank in ------------- Country		Period of R Return with which the realisation has been reported to RBI
		In our name	In the name of *--- ------------------------	Held with us	Held with * --- ------------------	
(1)	(2)	(3)	(4)	(5)	(6)	(7)

2. AR-1 form :
Application for Removal of Excisable goods on payment of duty

Central Excise Series No. 57

Original
Duplicate
Triplicate

NOTES :- (i)] Where additional excise duty is also leviable, separate entries for basic and additional excise duties should be made on different horizontal lines and the amounts totalled. Separate entries should similarly be made in columns 1,3 and 4 of Part I of the Statement of duty paid (on the reverse).

[(ii)] 'Real value' is the value referred to in section 4 of the [Central Excise Act,1944.]

(iii) 'Invoice value is the value specified by the manufacturer or producer to the customer. This value should be given in all classes.

(iv) 'Tariff value' is the value fixed by the Central Government under section 3 of the Central Excises and Salt Act,1944. This column should be filled in wherever applicable.]

Assessment Memorandum

(To be entered in words and figures)
1. Total number of packages..
2. Quantity of goods on which duty is assessed............................
3. Rate of duty...
4. Total duty payable..
Signature............................
................of Central Excises

Place...................
Date...........................

Statement of duty paid at............

Declaration

I/We declare the above particulars to be true and correctly stated.

I/We apply for leave to clear the above goods.

....
Signature of the owner or his authorised agent

Place........................
Date.....................

<u>Treasury</u>
<u>Sub-Treasury</u>
<u>State Bank of India</u>
<u>Reserve Bank of India</u>

I. *For payment in cash*
(To be filled in by the owner or his authorised agent.)

Name of person tendering payment	Name and address of person on whose behalf the amount is tendered	Particulars of payment	Amount Rs. Ps.	Head of Account
1	2	3	4	5

(1) Excise duty on* 038— UNION EXCISE DUTIES]
(2) **Additional Duties of Excise under the Additional Duties of Excise
    (Goods of Special Importance) Act, 1957:—

Textiles — Cotton/Woollen/Silk/Artificial Silk,
Tobacco — Unmanufactured Tobacco/Cigarettes/Cigars and Cheroots, Sugar
(in words) Rupees...Total
Date............................. Signature of tenderer...
Deposit Number : (To be filled in by Treasury or Bank)
  Certificate
  Received payment of rupees..(in words)
  Signature of Treasurer...
  Accountant...
Date Treasury Officier...
  Agent or Manager...

II. For payment through Current Account

Title of Account or Ledger number	Number and date of entry	Amount Rs. P.

Date...................................... Signature of the owner or his authorised agent

III. For payment by Money Order

Number and date of Money Order (Receipt to be attached to original application)	Amount Rs. P.

Date......................................Clearance allowed Signature of the owner or his authorised agent
Number and Date of transport permit,if any Signature..
Date... ....of Central Excise
* Here enter name of commodity ** to be cancelled where inapplicable *** unnecessary words to be scored out

3. AR-4 form :
Application for removal of excisable goods for export by (Air/Sea/Port/Land)

Central Excise Series No. 60
Central Excise Series No. 60-A

EXPORT UNDER VBAL/QBAL/OTHERS
A.R.4No..............

Original (White)
Duplicate (Buff)
Triplicate (Pink)
Quadruplicate (Green)
Quintuplicate (Blue)
Sixtuplicate (Yellow)

Range..........
Division.............Address....................
Collectorate...................

FORM A.R. 4
Application for removal of excisable goods for export by (Air/Sea/Port/Land)*

To

    Superintendent of Central Excise
    ....(Full Postal Address)

    1. Particulars of [Asstt. Commissioner of Central Excise]/Maritime Commissioner of Central Excise from whom rebate shall be claimed/with whom bond is executed and his complete postal address.

    2. I/We .... of ....propose to export the under-mentioned consignment to .... (Country of destination) by Air/Sea/Land/Parcel Post under claim for rebate/bond*.

Particulars of Manufacturer of goods-and his Central Excise Reg. No.	No. and Description of packages	Gross weight/Net weight	Marks and Nos. on packages	Quantity of goods	Description of goods
(1)	(2)	(3)	(4)	(5)	(6)

Value Rs.P	Duty		No. and date of Invoice under which duty was paid/No. and date of bond executed under Rule 13*	Amount of Rebate claimed	Remarks
	Rate Rs.P.	Amt. Rs.P.			
(7)	(8)	(9)	(10)	(11)	(12)

    3. I/We hereby certify that the above- mentioned goods have been manufactured.
    a) availing facility/without availing facility of Modvat credit under Rule 57A, Rule 57Q of Central Excise Rules, 1944.
    (b) availing facility/without availing facility under Rule 12(I)(b) of Central Excise Rules, 1944.
    (c) availing facility/without availing facility under Rule 13(I)(b) of Central Excise Rules, 1944.

    4. I/We hereby declare that the export is in discharge of the export obligation under a Quantity based Advance Licence/Value based Advance Licence/Under Claim of Duty Drawback under Customs & Central Excise Duties Drawback Rules, 1971 *.

    5. I/We hereby declare that the above particulars are true and correctly stated.

Time of Removal................................. Signature of owner or his authorised
agent with date.
Name in Block Letters & Designation
SEAL

PART A
CERTIFICATION BY THE CENTRAL EXCISE OFFICER

1. Certified that duty has been paid on the goods described overleaf by debit entry in the Personal Ledger Account No. ..../RG 23A (Pt. II) NO......../RG 23B (Pt. II) No......... against Excise Invoice No............. dated ..../that the owner has entered into B1/B16 bond No. .... under Rule 13/14 of Central Excise Rules, 1944 with the.............................

2. Certified that I have opened and examined the packages No............. and found that the particulars stated and the description of goods given overleaf read with the invoice and the packing list (if any) correct (and that all the packages have been stuffed in the container No. .... with Marks ....) and the same has been sealed with Central Excise Seal/One Time Seal (OTS) No. ....

3. I have verified with the records, the certificate of the owner given in Sl. No. 3 overleaf regarding non-availability of benefits under rule 57A, 57Q, 12(1) (a)/13(1) (b) and found it to be true.

4. Certified that I have drawn three representative samples from the consignment and have handed over, two sets thereof duly sealed to the exporter/his authorised representative.

Place.....................
Date ....

Signature Signature
(Name in Block Letters) (Name in Block Letters)
Superintendent of Central Excise Inspector of Central Excise

PART B

CERTIFICATION BY THE CUSTOMS OFFICER

Certified that the consignment was shipped under my supervision under Shipping Bill No............. dated............ by S-S./Flt No............ which left on the............ day of..........19.......

OR

Certified that the above mentioned consignment has been duly identified and has passed the land frontier today at............ in its original condition under Bill of Exports No...

Place..................
Date...................

Signature
(Name and designation of the Customs
Officer in Block Letters)
(Seal)

NOTE----The customs officer shall send the duplicate to the address given at Sl. No. 1 overleaf and hand over original and

Sixtuplicate to the exporter.

PART C
EXPORT BY POST

Certified that the consignment described overleaf has been despatched by foreign post to.................. on........... day of.................................... 19...............

Place..........................
Date..............................

Signature of Post Master
(Seal)

PART D
REBATE SANCTION ORDER

(On Original, Duplicate and Triplicate)

Refund Order No......... dated............. Rebate ofRs............ (Rupees.............) sanctioned vide cheque No............. dated ....

Place ....　　　　　　　　　　　　　　　Assistant Commissioner/ Maritime
Date.....................　　　　　　　　　　　　　　　Commissioner of Central Excise